Postmark Collecting

R. K. FORSTER

Postmark Collecting

STANLEY PAUL

London

STANLEY PAUL & CO. LTD

178–202 Great Portland Street, London, W.1

  AN IMPRINT OF THE   HUTCHINSON GROUP

London Melbourne Sydney
Auckland Bombay Toronto
Johannesburg New York

 ★

First published 1960

*This book has been set in Times type
face. It has been printed in Great Britain on
Antique Wove paper by Taylor Garnett
Evans & Co. Ltd., Watford, Herts., and
bound by them*

To

That loyal and tolerant team

HEATHER, JOHN & CLARE

Acknowledgements

THE Author wishes gratefully to acknowledge his indebtedness:

To the Director of the Bureau International de L'Union Postale Universelle, Berne, Switzerland, for information and statistical data;

To the Public Relations Department, General Post Office, London, and the Public Relations Department (Post Office) North East Region, for practical help and advice;

To Messrs. W. & R. Chambers, Limited, for permission to reproduce passages from *The Postmark on a Letter*;

To Miss Kathleen Partridge for generously allowing the use of her poem from the series *Just A Thought*;

AND

To the tireless co-operation and helpfulness of fellow-collectors, friends, and officials in the postal services of many nations throughout the world's far corners who, for many years, have patiently helped to harvest much of the material upon which this book is based.

Contents

Just a Thought

THE postmark on a letter always means so much
to me. It is a tiny circle into which I seem to see – a
place, a time, a person, a purpose and a thought,
plus the intervening towns through which the letter
has been brought.

I sometimes read a postmark and I see a village
street, a footpath through the meadows and a pond
where ducklings meet. A little cottage garden, or a
busy market square and I gather in old memories
and breathe the fragrant air. I sometimes see a
picture of the pebbles on the beach, of boats and
fishermen and lofty cliffs far out of reach.

And sometimes it is just a picture of a city
street, of people hurrying to work where shops and
crossroads meet. Of machinery and typewriters, of
papers, pens and ink, of lives that link . . . and of
the one who wrote to me I think.

All from a tiny postmark, such a very ample
view, whether of something old and sweet or
something near and new.

KATHLEEN PARTRIDGE

By Way of Introduction

MOST people are inclined to take postmarks pretty much for granted. 'What is the postmark?' we may ask when someone tells us there is a letter in unrecognized handwriting waiting for us beside the toast-rack. We are not really interested. What we mean, ninety-nine times out of a hundred, is 'Who is the letter from?' We merely ask about the postmark to short-circuit the mental game of Twenty Questions about who can have written to us.

This is a pity.

Postmarks, once you begin to take an interest in them, are a fascinating subject, informative and stimulating: a challenge to one's dormant sense of surprise. During the course of their long and intriguing history they have been responsible for many things. They have convicted criminals and they have broken marriages; they have caused misunderstandings, and prevented them. They have been collected by peers and forged by swindlers. They have featured in lawsuits and in television plays and on countless occasions they have proved and disproved the value of philatelic treasures. They have, on various pretexts, been commended and condemned and they have, with impersonal candour, caused happiness and heartache, laughter and tears.

In spite of all this postmarks remain one of the commonest commonplaces of our everyday lives and, as such, they have been taken for granted by every generation familiar with them since Colonel Henry Bishop, Postmaster-General in the reign of Charles II, introduced them to England in 1661.

Oddly enough it is only in relatively recent years that postmarks have to any great extent attracted the attention of collectors. In Britain as far back as the late 1860s certain enthusiasts, among the earliest of them a certain Mr. Thomas Gosse, of Bath, derived pleasure from their interest in the subject, but not until 1883 did the idea of forming a club take shape. In that year a group of collectors, about twenty in number, succeeded in uniting to form what is now known as the Postmark Club.

In the United States of America records indicate that postmarks have been systematically collected for almost one hundred years. The method in the beginning was similar to that used by philatelists today. Postmarks (usually round) were cut from envelopes and cards and then glued into suitably marked and arranged pages in books.

Today some tens of thousands of people in Britain and abroad are keen and enthusiastic postmark collectors. To meet this large and growing interest in the subject specialist societies such as the Postmark Club, the British Postmark Society, the Travelling Post Office and Seapost Society, the Postal History Society, the American Maritime Postmark Society and the United States Cancellation Club have been established with members in more than twenty-five countries.

The reasons for the astonishing popularity of the postmark as the subject for a collector's hobby are not far to seek. There is much more behind the date-stamp on a letter than the mere fact that it might have been imprinted with the hurried impartiality of a 900-letters-a-minute stamp-cancelling machine or with the careful precision of a rural sub-postmistress at the grocery store post office near the village green.

First, there are the historical associations of old specimens that signpost the way back through years that have long ago slipped away into old, forgotten silences.

'Intreat Mr. Dronning to convey this saiffley by the post . . .'

'To my loveing Friend Richard Leethe, at Gowle Court in the parishe of Great Malverne some 4 miles from Worcester & about halfe a mile of Cleveloade . . .'

'For John Rushworth, Esquire, at a groicer's shoppe nexte White Beare in Old Southampton Buildings, over against Graise Inn Gate . . .'

These, and their like, are postal superscriptions that have survived the centuries on letters conveyed by Royal Messengers 'ridynge in all dyllygent haste' along rutted roads infested with prowling footpads and lurking highwaymen.

In their letters the collector may 'touch the hand of poets', read the private hopes of statesmen and share the fears of common folk as they set to paper in bygone days ambitions and yearnings and hopes and confusions that, once, were important to them. For envelopes, though they were used in France in the seventeenth century, were not common in England until after the introduction of the Penny Postage system in 1840. It follows that many of the older postal markings are imprinted on the letters themselves: letters folded and sealed by the fingers of

14

statesmen, beauties, poets, travellers, truants, and tyrants in forgotten yester-years.

Some of these letters, like the clipped conversation of passers-by on a city street, are tantalizingly incomplete. Others are poignantly whole, spotlighting with black and white clarity some moment of time that was living and warm before life swept on and left behind only a collector's piece.

But our concern is as much with the surprising oddities of recent years as with these fascinating cameos from bygone days.

Modern postmarks have been issued from ships, hotels, palaces, airports, schools, exhibitions, trains, hospitals, and prisons. There was once a special postmark for the Royal Yacht, as there was for Captain Scott's tragic expedition to the South Pole.

'Posted On Bridge During Opening Celebrations' was the inscription on letters posted on Sydney Harbour Bridge, Australia, in 1932, and 'Sea Floor, Bahamas' was the imprint of the world's first undersea post office established in the Williamson Photosphere on the sea floor off the Bahamas in 1939. Major exhibitions in places as widely separated as New York, Paris, Vienna, Philadelphia, and Melbourne, geographical features such as Table Mountain and Niagara Falls, and feats of human endurance on land and sea and in the air have all, at various times, been commemorated in the form of postal date-stamps.

My personal interest in this fascinating hobby began in 1932, when I was seventeen. I began to collect the postmarks of Yorkshire, and I kept them in a shoe-box. Since then I have managed to accumulate 25,000 postal date-stamps from cities and seaports and tucked-away places in every corner of the globe.

Twenty-five thousand postmarks!

They have congregated, these humble black imprints, in my carefully catalogued files after journeying by land and sea and air from the world's far corners. Within my files are date-stamps from Iceland and from Chile, from China and Ceylon, from Monaco and Madagascar, from the Yukon and the South Pacific islands. And by the time one has accumulated 25,000 postal date-stamps one has learnt quite a lot. Not only about postmarks, but about people and places, too!

Goodness knows how many overseas friends I have who periodically send me material. Their number is legion. There is Jan in the Netherlands and Ellen in Panama. There is Mr. Albert Burden, in Australia, who occasionally goes 'walkabout' and sends me postal date-stamps from the exotic places he visits. There is Mr. J. C. Webster, of Winter

Haven, Florida, who, for years, has devoted many hours a week to his self-imposed task of keeping the American section of my collection well supplied with material, and there is Frank Park, of Vancouver, Canada, who gathers from his business friends and overseas' correspondents exciting batches of material they would otherwise discard.

There is Erna, Raynell, Hugo, and Carlos – and there is even Hidekiti, in Japan. I do not know whether that is his first name or his second name. He writes earnestly, in green ink on rice paper and he is kind enough to translate for me from the Japanese characters the place-names of the date-stamps he sends. Then there is Demetrios, in Athens. He sends me postmarks of Corfu and Patras and his letters whisper, if letters may whisper, of the peerless white Parthenon in the blue and gold of an Athenian summer.

From these sources, and from many others, I derive my main supply of new and fascinating material, so the arrival of the postman at my home is always an event full of delightful hope and speculation.

In my search for unusual postmarks I come across places bearing strange and sometimes beautiful names. Honeymoon, Heart's Delight, Paradise, and Beauty. Bowlegs, Badlot, Bumble Bee, and Banana. I find imprints from wild, improbable places: Cut and Shoot, Bung Bong, Wait-a-Bit, Fireworks, and Freezywater. I find myself wondering who christened Peculiar and what is so wildly funny about Ha! Ha! Bay. I speculate about Sleepy Eye and wonder what happened at Accident. I smile at Shickshinny and shudder at Shivers and wonder who gave Go Home its inhospitable name.

The world is full of places with names as intriguing as these and whenever I receive a postmark 'queeriosity' with a name like Mumps, What Cheer, or Double Head Cabbage, it immediately sets me map-wandering to discover where it came from.

This, then, is part of the pattern and part of the fun of postmark collecting. Not the whole of the pattern, not the whole of the fun: for the pattern is constantly changing and the fun is unending.

In the pages to come I have set out in word and picture some of the highlights of the postmark hobby and some of the outstanding oddities that have come my way during more than a quarter of a century of active collecting.

In Part One of this book I have attempted to outline for you the broad background picture of the postmark-collecting pastime and suggest some ways in which you might start a collection of your own.

In Part Two I have tried to present in alphabetical sequence – which

16

enables you to pick where you please – some notes about postmarks, places, and people.

You may choose, in Part Two, to begin a worldwide 'tour' with a trip to the ocean bed by reading about that seven-day wonder, the Sea Floor Post Office, which existed briefly on the sea floor off Nassau. You may choose to end your trip way up in the mountains of Peru by reading about the sky-high post office of Cerro de Pasco, reputedly the highest permanent post office in the world.

You may wish to begin by reading about Royal postmarks, about the town that took its name from an American television show, about collectors' clubs, or about the Mole Hill that became a Mountain.

The choice is yours. They are all in this book. And whenever it has been possible to do so I have provided postmark illustrations to prove that truth is, indeed, often stranger than fiction.

Whatever your choice, wherever you begin, I hope that in the pages to come you will find pleasure and interest and that, finally, when you set down this book you may be tempted to discover, as I have discovered, that there is fun and fascination to be found in the satisfying hobby of Postmark Collecting.

PART ONE

1
A Hobby with a History

WE might begin by asking: What *is* a postmark?

Most dictionaries define the word as 'a mark or stamp of a post office on a letter'. To this definition the more erudite works may add a word or two of functional description. Thus: 'A mark stamped by post office officials on letters, etc., usually stating place, date and hour of dispatch, and serving to deface the postage stamp.'

With this definition of a modern postmark we may be satisfied. It would be wise, however, to emphasize that the earliest postal date-stamps failed in three ways to conform to this general description. They stated neither the place nor the hour of dispatch, and, since they preceded even the famous Victorian Penny Black adhesive postage stamp by nearly one hundred and eighty years, it follows that their earliest services did not include the defacement of postage stamps.

When, and by whom, were postmarks first devised?

Their beginnings, according to some sources, are lost in the mists of obscurity. Postmarked letters written 5,000 years ago by Court officials in the time of the Third Dynasty are on view in an Egyptian museum. These postal markings, in red or blue, show the place of the letter's origin and bear the slogan, 'In the name of the living King, speed!'

In 1945 a letter tablet of the Babylonian Era (1900 B.C.), written, or impressed, on baked brick and relating to a business transaction and a debt due, was offered for sale by auction in a London saleroom. The valuation placed upon this rare item was £15.

But postmarks, in a form recognizable as such today, made their appearance, in England, at a much later date: in 1661. Up to that year the only postal markings on letters were handwritten, the principal purpose of such markings being to indicate the amount of postage paid or due. Only rarely were the dates of posting entered except in the case

21

of urgent letters on State business. These frequently had recorded upon them a complete time-table of arrivals and departures along the postal route, together with the time of ultimate delivery, and, sometimes, on the front of the letter the drawing in conventional outline of a gallows as a warning to those who might be tempted to waylay the mail and an injunction to the carrier to 'Haste, Post – Haste for Lyfe!'

Soon after the Restoration the Postmaster-General, Colonel Henry Bishop, stated in reply to charges of postal delays:

'A Stamp is invented, that is putt upon every letter shewing the day of the moneth that every letter comes to the office, so that no Letter Carryer may dare detayne a letter from post to post, which before was usual. . . .'

In this way, with something of a flourish, and with this naïve condemnation of the seventeenth-century postal service to justify its use, the birth of the postmark was announced.

Further confirmation of the event would appear to be provided by an official post office announcement which appeared in the news-sheet *Mercurius Publicus*, dated 25 April to 2 May, 1661. In this it was stated:

'. . . and to prevent any neglect of the Letter-carriers in the speedy delivery of letters from the said Office: It is notifyed that the days of recept of every Letter at the Office is printed upon the Letter and the Letter-carriers ought to deliver them the same day in the summer: and the next morning at farthest in the winter: and if any fayler be complained of at the Post Office it shall be redressed. . . .'

To Colonel Henry Bishop, then, as Postmaster-General, is given the credit for the 'invention' of postmarks. It is reasonably certain, however, that Bishop was not personally responsible for the innovation. He was a new-comer to postal work, having assumed office only in 1660 as a 'farmer' or contractor at a rental of £21,500 a year for seven years. Moreover, Bishop's association with the office was of only short duration. Before three years had passed he surrendered his lease and was succeeded for the remainder of his term by Colonel Daniel O'Neale, or O'Neile, 'Groom of the King's Bedchamber'. In 1663 the revenues of the post office, subject to a substantial payment to the king, were settled on the Duke of York and, at his accession as James II, they reverted to the Crown.

The original suggestion regarding the use of date-stamps probably derived from the promptings of experienced post office officials who had served under Cromwell's Commonwealth, and possibly before, under Charles I.

To whomever the credit should go, the fact remains that at this time and in this way postmarks were officially employed in England, their primary purpose being defined in the succinct phrase '. . . so that no Letter-carryer may dare detayne a letter from post to post. . . .'

So far as is known no example of the actual Bishop handstamp (that is, the device used to make the impression) is in existence. The method of assembly is therefore not known with certainty, though there is evidence to suggest that the die, or head, was in a solid unit inserted into a wooden haft containing date units which were changed daily.

In appearance the date-stamp impressions themselves were simple in the extreme. They consisted merely of a circle thirteen millimetres in diameter divided horizontally by a line. In the top half of the semi-circle were placed letters denoting the month, while the lower half enclosed numerals representing the day of the month. The year, at this stage, was not shown.

Known to collectors today as 'Bishop Marks' these pioneer date-stamps were used, at first exclusively, in London, Edinburgh, Dublin, and in the British colonies of North Africa and India.

Provincial place-marks, the first of which appeared about the year 1700, were slow to follow the lead of London's 'Bishop Marks' in the matter of incorporating the date. With the exception of Bristol where, in 1705, a curious imprint in the form of a 'B' (with date and month in the loops) made its appearance, most provincial centres used a simple undated straight-line imprint.

About the year 1750, under the provisions of the numerous Turnpike Acts which were being passed, the trustees of the roads were required to measure distances and set up milestones. A result of this was that distances, as reckoned by the post office in computing charges for the carriage of mail, were often found to be considerably under the true figures. As soon as the milestones were in place the charges for horses and for letters were adjusted, and to assist in applying the increased rates the mileages from London began to appear on the postmarks imprinted by country offices. In an extensive check carried out by the post office over sixty years later many of these mileages were found to be incorrect and postmasters at the centres concerned were directed to file off the mileage figures.

About the year 1786 an important alteration was made in the date-stamps of London. For the first time an imprint was used which gave the date in full including numerals representing the year. In 1794, and for a year or two later, a number of experimental types of handstamps were introduced in displacement of the Bishop model. These new handstamps combined such words as 'Paid', 'Post Paid', or 'Postage Paid' with letters and numerals representing the day, month, and year held in concentric rings, and fully interchangeable. The first type was square but it was discovered that the corners of the handstamp tore the letters when a level 'strike' was not secured. To remedy this the corners of the handstamps were chamfered, but presumably the trouble persisted and eventually round or oval date-stamps were adopted as standard until machine cancellation was introduced.

Thus, gradually, the postmark progressed through the various stages of its development towards the form familiar today until, with the general introduction of adhesive postage stamps – on 6 May 1840 – the important new function of stamp cancellation supplemented its original function.

Behind these bare details lies an enthralling field of research into the early rites and duties of the post office. It is a colourful field. A sphere in which move the personalities of little-known pioneers. We meet Sir Brian Tuke, 'Master of the Messengers and Runners', who in 1533 observed that some people, in order to discredit the postal service, pre-dated their letters by two or three days and blamed the service when the letters were delivered apparently late. We encounter William Dockwra, a merchant, who in 1683 devised a new penny postal system in London, characterized by a heart-shaped handstruck 'hour stamp', a pioneer alternately favoured and persecuted by the authorities, and we are introduced to Peter Williamson, Dockwra's Edinburgh counterpart, whose penny postal service of 1774 had its distinctive 'paid' and 'unpaid' stamps. We hear about John Rea, 'receiver of letters', the first known stamper of letters, and find postal date-stamp evidence of the existence of Mrs. Grove 'at the Temple Gates in the Strand', who pioneered in a humble, anonymous way the registration of mail with her peculiar postmark – the letter 'G' in a dotted circle.

Ship letters – packet letters – the Free Franking system – Penny Blacks and Mulready envelopes. These form part of the muddled and marvellous patchwork of Britain's postal history.

Into this sphere the collector of pre-postage stamp material may wander at will, lured into enchanting by-ways by each new acquisition. With the yellowing manuscript letter before him he may share, for example, the apprehension of Lady Mary Roche as she writes under the date-line 'Dublin, 24 September 1798, to her brother at Thirkleby House, near York: 'Sir Boyle and I had a very good journey and on our arrival at Chester we were electrified by the news of another French invasion . . .' and the collector may be 'electrified', too, by the use of so modern a word in so old a setting.

Upon the specialist collector the pioneer date-stamps of overseas countries are liable, also, to press their urgent claims. France, where postmarks made their appearance in 1695, is a fascinating field; Austria, whose postal imprints – those of Vienna – were introduced in 1751, is another; the United States of America, home of the romantic Pony Express and the Mississippi mail boats, where the early date-stamps followed independent lines of erratic shape and content; the Bahamas, where postmarks were introduced in 1802, and Denmark, late in the field, where date-stamps had their beginnings in 1851 and each post office had to provide its own cancelling ink – with consequent opportunity for the dishonest to 'clean' their stamps and use them again.

For the specialist collector these fields lie waiting: fresh fields, many of them, charged with the delights of pioneer research and the incomparable thrill of discovery. For in the realm of postal history much is still unrevealed.

But not all of us have the time, the opportunity or the means to pursue so pleasurable a pastime. For if the rewards of research are infinite so, too, are the labours and for the average enthusiast they are prohibitive.

The collection of very early material of postal history interest is fascinating and rewarding. But no less so is the gathering of modern material in a realistic and systematic way and this is the field to which most new-comers to the hobby are attracted.

We begin by looking back. We have traced, if briefly, the historical background of postal markings through centuries of sculptured calm and violent upheaval. It was necessary to do this because the person who derives the greatest pleasure from any collecting hobby is he who gathers his material in the light of what he knows or can discover by research or inquiry. The genuine enthusiast in any sphere is seldom content merely to amass a collection of kindred objects. He must go forward, probing, questioning, gathering facts and seeking knowledge. For the flame of curiosity, once kindled, is not easily extinguished and from this heightened sense of awareness of the romance and challenging possibilities of his subject the collector may gain much in pleasure and accumulated knowledge.

So we begin by looking back: by glancing at the background story of a hobby that remembers History and with which forgotten fragments of other people's lives are inseparably associated.

And now, after our brief excursion into the realm of postal history, let us set out together to discover some answers to the question: 'Why collect postmarks?'

2

Why Collect Postmarks?

MANY motives prompt people to collect things.

Covetousness, the desire to possess something unique, the love of hoarding, the urge to acquire knowledge, a sense of genuine interest in the subject – these are but a few among the multitude of reasons why, at one time or another, most of us discover there is a curious fascination in gathering together a number of objects of one kind.

In the hobby of postmark collecting most of these motives, and many more besides, are adequately catered for. The dividend of pleasure and interest is exceptionally high and the scope of the subject is as wide and varied as the collector wishes to make it.

For a start, postmarks are comparatively easy to come by and as much modern material has virtually no market value an interesting collection can be gathered at little cost.

Apart from these considerations the postmark hobby has much to commend it. It teaches one, for instance, a good deal about geography – and history, in the postal history sense. One seldom obtains a specimen from some out-of-the-way place without pursuing a desire to know more about the date-stamp's place of origin and since the history of postmarks goes back such a long way one is often tempted to explore the fascinating by-ways of postal history.

In this way the hobby keeps alert the collector's senses of inquiry and discovery.

The hobby tends, also, to make infinitely more interesting the journeys one may undertake. A walking-tour, for example, could enrich one's collection considerably if a self-addressed postcard were to be dispatched from some of the intriguing places one visits in this way and trips to new and exciting places are recalled for years to come by the postal date-stamps (giving the date and place of the visit) gathered 'in the field' and placed in one's collection.

The harvesting and filing and 'writing up' of material has beneficial effects. It trains the collector to be neat and orderly in his methods, for merely to collect material is not enough; it must be arranged and presented in a satisfactory and pleasing way.

Inevitably, the postmark hobby leads to the forming of many fine friendships with fellow-collectors and with friends at home and overseas. It is, indeed, surprising how willing and eager people are to assist in a collecting hobby of this kind once the enthusiast's needs are known. From far and near letters and inquiries will come from helpers who are keen to add new material to the growing collection and so, in its own small way, the hobby tends to promote friendship and international fellowship and goodwill.

It is a hobby that is especially good for invalids or for those who are living, by preference or obligation, in remote and out-of-the-way places with few social and entertainment facilities.

Beyond these considerations lies the personal thrill of adventure and discovery: of exploring new horizons and acquiring contact with strange and intriguing places in the world's far corners. For postmarks, by their very nature, are part of the modern world's miraculous chain of communication. About them, too, is the ring of authenticity: they carry, as a certificate of birth, the date and time and place of their origin. The adhesive postage stamp in mint condition in the philatelist's album may have travelled no farther afield than the printing press in London: it may not have been postally used in the country whose name it may bear.

But a postmark bears beyond reasonable contradiction the very impression of authenticity. It suggests the lure of distant places, the extravagant hint of far horizons, the zest of postal exploration and, perhaps, in a vicarious way, the effortless thrill of foreign travel.

For the collector in this field there are no frontiers. The limpid heat of Equatorial seaports or the chill silences of Arctic wastes may be suggested by date-stamps from Mombasa or the vast spaces of Alaska.

With the postmark to spotlight his interest in the place the collector may discover the story of the mole-hill that became a mountain: how, in fact, the inhabitants of Mole Hill, West Virginia, decided to change the name of their home-town and chose, with hilarious apposition, the new name – Mountain. He may learn, and record as an item of interest, that the township of Goodnight, New South Wales, derived its name from the greeting of a lonely man on a bend of the Murray River and he may learn that Faith is in Canada, Hope in Alaska, and Charity, biblically the greatest of these, is located in the state of Missouri, U.S.A.

It is in the acquisition of material of this sort that the answer to the question, 'Why collect postmarks?' is most readily found, for collecting postmarks is rather like embarking upon a personal voyage of adventure and discovery and the traveller can never be quite sure where the journey will end.

3

How to Start a Collection

How should one begin to build a collection of postmarks? To this question there is no quick, specific answer. So much depends on the collector's opportunities, the particular sphere of his interest and the ability of friends and fellow-collectors to assist in the search for material. Some general advice may suggest a few of the many ways in which material can be obtained and it is often true that, once a start has been made, one's fellow enthusiasts and friends are only too glad to help.

For the collector of pre-1840 material the field is largely restricted to specimens obtainable through dealers, attendance at philatelic auctions, membership of a collectors' club or through private channels. There are, for example, a number of dealers and firms specializing in specific categories of material such as those connected with aerophilately or the postal history of Great Britain. The advertisement columns of the philatelic Press will suggest many outlets of this type through which the nucleus of a collection can be created.

Occasionally that varying fortune which sometimes enables the philatelist to acquire for a trifling sum material of great value will similarly smile upon the postmark collector. Old letters bearing interesting postmarks have, for instance, sometimes been discovered between the leaves of books where they have lain forgotten for years. General dealers who buy household bric-à-brac are another surprising source from which old correspondence bearing precious postal imprints can occasionally be brought to light. The lumber rooms of country houses and the archives of legal offices are further sources for the discovery of hoarded documents and, since these are often worthless to their possessors, they can often be obtained for the asking.

From these sources and from the generosity of friends and collectors, the student of early postal date-stamps may hope to gather material to begin and, later develop, his collection.

For the collector of modern date-stamps – and this is the category to which the interest of most young people is readily attracted – the opportunities for gathering specimens are greatly increased. Almost every family has a circle of friends and correspondents and from these one may gather the first items with which to form a collection.

But soon the enthusiast will have to go farther afield, and here the exercise of a little ingenuity will help. Among the postage stamps in most stamp collectors' duplicates will be found, for example, many which bear interesting postmarks. So the opportunities for 'trading' stamps for postmarks must not be overlooked. Missionary packets, sold by weight and obtainable from stamp dealers, are another source of material.

Still another rich store-room in which post-1840 postmarks are to be found are the albums of picture postcards amassed by collectors of earlier days. During the past fifty years or so thousands of varieties of picture postcards have been issued and literally millions of these have passed through the post since their first appearance, in Britain, in 1894. For most people the craze for collecting picture postcards has waned, yet in the attics and store-rooms of hundreds of homes are lodged albums between whose dusty covers are postcards bearing many first-class postal imprints.

Nor should it be imagined that postmark collecting is a strictly indoor pastime. Reference to how a walking-tour at home or abroad could enrich one's collection has already been made. But cycling tours or motor trips with the family could be equally productive if an addressed postcard were to be dispatched from some of the places one visits in this way and if one's personal movements are restricted the co-operation of friends who are journeying to interesting places can often be enlisted.

Overseas correspondents are an obvious source of specimens from abroad. Quite apart from the enjoyable and often lasting friendships thus made, such correspondents are often most helpful in supplying unusual date-stamps and information which might otherwise be unobtainable.

Letters to the magazine and newspaper Press on the subject of one's hobby often bring a shoal of exciting specimens into the collector's net. Evidence of this is provided by a Yorkshire grammar school boy who wrote to the editor of a Sunday newspaper giving details of some of the outstanding examples comprising his curious postal place-names collection. Within a short time the writer of this letter was virtually bombarded with missives from far and near, many of them enclosing postmarks believed by their senders to rival in oddity the claims of those named in the newspaper.

Esperantists and friends in businesses with wide overseas connections can be of great assistance. The former, unhampered by linguistic barriers, are often prolific correspondents on a world-wide scale; the latter frequently have access to a collector's treasure chest of discarded envelopes from every quarter of the globe.

Finally, but by no means least, membership of one or more of the growing number of societies catering for various branches of the hobby may be cited as an admirable means of enlarging the albums and the knowledge of the enthusiast who is sufficiently serious in his interest to be accepted as a member.

Practically every philatelic society – and they are world-wide and numerous – has its devotees of the postmark hobby. But several societies exist either largely or exclusively for enthusiasts in this branch.

Among clubs within this category, to some of which reference has already been made, are the Postmark Club (established 1883), the British Postmark Society (formed in 1958), the Travelling Post Office and Seapost Society (maritime and railway postmarks), the American Maritime Postmark Society (founded in 1939), the Postal History Society (inaugurated in 1936), the (American) Postmark Collectors' Club (founded 1943), the United States Cancellation Club and the International Stamp and Hobby Society – these having, among them, several thousand members in over twenty-five different countries of the world. Departments of these societies include those of exchange (of specimens and information), research, sales and advice. By many of them bulletins are issued and most of the societies mentioned organize the exchange of material among members, who range in status from baronet to baker and in age from teenager to octogenarian.

The growth and development of these societies may, indeed, be some indication of the rapid and widespread extension of interest in a hobby which, in Britain and America in the 1860's, claimed as far as is recorded a mere handful of active devotees.

These, then, are some of the ways in which a collection may be started. There are many others. Opportunities, obviously, will vary according to the degree of enterprise and activity evinced by the collector.

32

4

Equipment Needed

A GOOD postmark collection deserves good accommodation.

This fact, superficially so apparent, is often overlooked or neglected by the enthusiastic beginner. A little thought, therefore, before one begins to adopt a particular method of housing and classifying one's collection may be well worth the trouble and will avoid the need for a drastic revision of one's methods at a later stage. It would, for example, clearly be absurd to waste time and effort and, perhaps, money in gathering material if the units comprising the collection were finally to be displayed in a careless and unworthy manner.

The first decision, then, may be – at least initially – to determine the limits of one's collecting activity. Having arrived at this decision the collector may next concern himself with a consideration of the most desirable method of housing his material.

On this subject opinions vary but upon certain fundamental matters most experienced collectors are unanimous. These may be summarized as follows:

Give your postmarks the dignity of space; do not cramp them by placing them too close together;

Use scissors only with the greatest care, remembering that a cut, once made, can never be unmade;

Never remove the postal markings from a first day cover or a cover likely to be of historical interest (in 1952 an envelope sold in auction for £775 because of its exotic postal markings: the two adhesive stamps on it, if removed from the envelope, were worth five shillings!);

Whenever possible, display the postmark and the postage stamp together. Combined in this way, the story they tell is given in greater detail;

Reject imperfect specimens – that is, postmarks which are smudged or dirty or which cannot readily be identified owing to imperfections;

Find out all you can about the places from which your postmarks originate;

Write up your collection in an attractive way so that each unit is made to contribute its share to the interest-value of the collection as a whole;

Allow plenty of space for the expansion of your collection;

Whenever possible, pass on to your fellow-collectors the knowledge you have gained concerning the hobby and be generous in your methods of exchange.

The eventual method of housing the collection is likely to be a matter of individual decision. Indeed, part of the attraction of the postmark hobby is that it has no tailor-made rules. Here, however, are some conventional methods which have the merits of simplicity and effectiveness.

First, the card index system.

This method is suitable for most types of collection except one consisting principally of complete envelopes or 'covers'. It is a handy, individual and convenient system and the cards can readily be adjusted to alphabetical, geographical or any other desired order of display.

To conform with the card index system date-stamps should be cut to a standard $4'' \times 2''$ size and should then be carefully stamp-hinged to plain white record cards about $5'' \times 3\frac{1}{2}''$ in size. A brief note regarding the place of origin may then be added in typescript or a clear style of handscript in the top left hand corner of the record card and on the reverse side of the card background facts (culled from newspaper items or a world gazetteer) can be noted regarding the postmark or its place of origin. The card index system allows for an unlimited degree of expansion and if the cards are accommodated in a number of boxes of suitable size, or in shallow drawers, they take up little space and can quickly be sorted into whatever sequence is desirable with the minimum amount of trouble and rearrangement.

Another method, suitable for the combined display of a group of collectors or as a 'visual aid' feature in a school classroom, is achieved by mounting the map of a country, county, province or other geographical division upon some suitably dark-surfaced material of paper, cloth or board. The background material should be made to overlap the edges of the map and upon this broad, dark margin may be displayed an attractive variety of postal date-stamps from towns and villages and centres of interest in the area covered by the map. A leader-tape may then be run from the postmark, in the margin, to the point on the map from which it derived. The tape should be firmly drawing-pinned at both ends so that the eye follows the line from postmark to map location.

An effective type of display can be arranged by using a loose-leaf album. These are obtainable in a great variety of shapes and sizes and it is merely necessary to give a group heading to each page of postmarks using, if desired, special printed 'titles of countries' gummed labels which can be bought from stamp dealers quite inexpensively and are arranged for cutting out and heading the blank pages of many types of postage stamp albums. To secure the specimens in an album of this kind, tags can be left above and below the postmarks when cutting them from the envelopes and the tags can be inserted into slits cut in the pages of the album. Alternatively, corner mounts of the type used in photographic albums can be employed.

A refinement of the loose-leaf method is the use of a large type of photograph album, about 10″ × 8″ in size, with *black* loose-leaf refill sheets. The dark background greatly enhances the appearance of the postmarks and if the specimens are neatly spaced the resultant display is extremely attractive.

Other useful accessories which may be briefly mentioned include a 4″ × 2″ plastic guide (to ensure uniformity when cutting postmarks from envelopes), a pair of spade-end tweezers for picking up individual postmarks, a plastic or glass magnifier for close scrutiny, a pocket wallet type of stock book (for carrying duplicates) and (a useful and relatively new accessory) a 'Philarule' gauge for accurately measuring the diameter of postmarks.

To assist him in identifying postmarks whose source of origin is obscure the collector has many aids. Guide books, including those published under the imprint of Karl Baedeker of Leipzig, maps and gazetteers will be an obvious channel for discovery of the location of out-of-the-way places; in addition there are many invaluable official publications.

Typical of these is the 700-page volume, *Post Offices in the United Kingdom*, issued by H.M. Postmaster-General and obtainable at most head post offices. This inexpensive book lists every post office in the United Kingdom excluding those covered by a companion volume, *London Post Offices and Streets*. Periodically amendments are issued to bring these volumes up to date. Similar publications are issued by the governments of Canada, Australia, the United States of America, France, Eire and many other territories. In the case of Eire a list is provided giving both the Irish form and the English form of Eireann place-names. Thus, for example, the place of origin of a date-stamp bearing the name 'Corcaigh' can readily be identified as 'Cork'.

Finally, but perhaps foremost in excellence from the viewpoint of the postmark collector, is the magnificent 1,500-page, two-volume publication, *Dictionnaire des Bureaux de Poste*, published in Berne, Switzerland, from the offices of the Universal Postal Union.

These volumes are almost literally a treasure house of intriguing fact and detail about the world's postal centres. In them are recorded details of post offices in every member-country of the Universal Postal Union. Iceland, Korea, Tanganyika, Tasmania – wherever the spotlight of one's attention may focus – these volumes have something entertaining to tell. From Wotton-under-Edge to Winneba, from Aabenraa, in Denmark to Zyyi, in Cyprus, calling at every link in the miraculous chain of world communication en route, this unique publication is the vehicle *par excellence* of entrancing journeys to strange and exotic lands.

As a means of postmark identification these two volumes are invaluable. More than that: they provide for the specialist in the date-stamps of any particular country a virtually complete catalogue of items to be sought.

In two separate spheres the beginner may experience difficulty in learning the history or place of origin of specimens coming into his possession. Old postal markings of the pre-stamp era may be one such source of trouble, and the postmarks deriving from obsolete offices another.

In the former field the collector is well served by the researches of philatelists and students of Postal History. The bibliography at the end of this book lists many works which cover in considerable detail the history of pre-stamp postmarks of Great Britain. The pre-stamp markings of other countries may present more complicated problems but, again, the answer is not far to seek. The postal authorities of most overseas countries will be found to be most helpful to the genuine seeker after knowledge. Many countries, in common with Great Britain, maintain efficient post office public relations departments from which an inquiry accompanied by the appropriate Commonwealth or International Reply Coupon will usually produce the information required.

Details of the postmarks of obsolete offices can often be obtained from old copies of the Post Office Guide which has been published for many years and used formerly to list the post offices in the United Kingdom. Reference may also be made to the secretaries of the many societies interested in the postmark collecting hobby.

PART TWO
Postmarks from A to Z

A

To an inconspicuous fishing village named Å in Åfjord canton, central Norway, goes the honour of heading the Universal Postal Union's formidable list of the world's half million post offices.

Apparently an industrious place (its industries are recorded as 'agriculture, lumbering, fishing and boat-building') the village of Å lies at the head of a fjord bearing its name, 36 miles north of Trondheim.

Its population is in the region of 2,500.

In the race to be, alphabetically speaking, the first postal place-name in the world there are many worthy contenders. Aabenraa, a seaport town of South Jutland, Denmark, is one of them; Aadorf, in Thurgau canton, Switzerland, is another. To another, smaller, Norwegian fishing village – Å i Lofoten – goes
the honour of second place. But in dictionaries and directories there are no dead heats: there are only outright winners.

And above is the winner's postmark portrait.

Abbreviations

Abbreviations, in postmark form, can be confusing to the collector who is not familiar with them. Here is a list of some territorial and postal abbreviations in current, or former, use on postmarks (as distinct from the many abbreviations in use on adhesive postage stamps):

A.C.T.	= Australian Capital Territory
A.E.F.	= French Equatorial Africa
A.F.B.	= Air Force Base
Ala.	= Alabama, U.S.A.
Alger.	= Algeria
Alpes Mmes.	= Alpes Maritimes, France

Alta.	= Alberta, Canada
Ang.	= Anglesey, Wales
Ann.	= Annex (U.S.A.)
A.P.O.	= Army Post Office.
Ariz.	= Arizona, U.S.A.
Ark.	= Arkansas, U.S.A.
A.Ruiz.	= Alfaro Ruiz, Costa Rica.
Atl.	= Atlantida, Honduras.
Aust.	= Australia.
B.A.	= Buenos Aires Province, Argentina.
B.C.	= British Columbia, Canada.
B.Cfa.	= Baja California, Mexico.
B.d.R.	= Bouches-du-Rhone, France.
Bech'd.	= Bechuanaland.
Beds.	= Bedfordshire, England.
Berks.	= Berkshire, England
B.F.P.O.	= British Forces Post Office
B.O.	= Branch Office
Bucks.	= Buckinghamshire, England.
B.W.I.	= British West Indies.
C.	= Catamarca Prov., Argentina.
Caern., Caerns.	= Caernarvonshire, Wales
Cal., Calif.	= California, U.S.A.
Cam.	= Campeche, Mexico.
Cambs.	= Cambridgeshire, England
Camg.	= Camguey, Cuba.
Cape.	= Cape Province, South Africa
Card., Cards.	= Cardiganshire, Wales.
Carm.	= Carmarthenshire, Wales.
Cba.	= Cordoba, Argentina.
C. du N.	= Côtes-du-Nord, France.
C.F.	= Federal Capital, Argentina.
C.G.H.	= Cape of Good Hope (obsolete).
C.H.	= Court House (U.S.A.)
Ches.	= Cheshire, England
Chih.	= Chihuahua, Mexico.
Chis.	= Chiapas, Mexico.
Ch.Is. or C.I.	= Channel Islands
Cho.	= Chaco, Argentina.
Cht.	= Chubut, Argentina.
C/K	= Cape Province, South Africa.
Coah.	= Coahuila, Mexico.
Co.Derry	= County Londonderry, Northern Ireland.
Co.Dur.	= Co. Durham, England.
Co. Ferm.	= Co. Fermanagh, Northern Ireland.
Col.	= Colima, Mexico.

Colo.	= Colorado, U.S.A.
Conn.	= Connecticut, U.S.A.
Ctgo.	= Cartago, Costa Rica.
Cts.	≐ Corrientes Province, Argentina.
Cumb., Cumbd.	= Cumberland, England.
Cwl., C'wall.	= Cornwall, England.
C.Z.	= Canal Zone.
D.C.	= District of Columbia, U.S.A.
Del.	= Delaware, U.S.A.
Denb., Denbs.	= Denbighshire, Wales.
D.F.	= Distrito Federal, Mexico.
Dgo.	= Durango, Mexico.
D.O.	= Delivery Office.
D.L.O.	= Dead Letter Office.
E.R.	= Entre Rios Province, Argentina.
F.	= Formosa Territory, Argentina.
F.D.C.	= First Day Cover.
Fla.	= Florida, U.S.A.
F.M.O.	= Fleet Mail Office (Canada).
F.M.S.	= Federated Malay States.
F.P.O.	= Field Post Office.
Ga.	= Georgia, U.S.A.
Glam.	= Glamorganshire, Wales.
Glos.	= Gloucestershire, England
G.M.C.R.	= Gobernación Militar de Comodoro, Argentina.
Gro.	= Guerrero, Mexico.
Gto.	= Guanajuato, Mexico
Hants.	= Hampshire. England.
Herefs.	= Herefordshire, England.
Herts.	= Hertfordshire, England.
Hgo.	= Hidalgo, Mexico.
H.P.O.	= Highway Post Office (U.S.A.)
Hte.	= Hautes (Alpes, Savoie, etc.) France.
Hunts.	= Huntingdonshire, England.
I. et V.	= Ille et Vilaine, France.
I.G.A.P.O.	= International Grenfell Association Post Office (Canada).
I.J.P.O.	= Imperial Japanese Post Office.
Ill.	= Illinois, U.S.A.
Ind.	= Indiana, U.S.A.
Ind. T.	= Indian Territory (now Oklahoma), U.S.A.
J.	= Jujuy Province, Argentina.
Jal.	= Jalisco, Mexico.

41

Kaap.	= Cape Province, South Africa.
Kans.	= Kansas, U.S.A.
Ky.	= Kentucky, U.S.A.
La.	= Louisiana, U.S.A.
Lanc., Lancs.	= Lancashire, England.
Leics.	= Leicestershire, England.
L. et C.	= Loir et Cher, France.
Lincs.	= Lincolnshire, England.
Loire Infre.	= Loire Inférieure, France.
L.P.	= La Pampa, Argentina.
L.R.	= La Rioja, Argentina.
Man.	= Manitoba, Canada.
Mass.	= Massachusetts, U.S.A.
M.B.	= *Boîte Mobile* ("Movable Box") q.v.
Md.	= Maryland, U.S.A.
Me.	= Maine, U.S.A.
Merth.	= Merionethshire, Wales
M. et L.	= Maine-et-Loire, France.
Mich.	= Michigan, U.S.A.; Michoacan, Mexico.
Middx., Mddx.	= Middlesex, England.
Minn.	= Minnesota, U.S.A.
Miss.	= Mississippi, U.S.A.
Mo.	= Missouri, U.S.A.
Mon.	= Monmouthshire.
Mont.	= Montgomeryshire, Wales; Montana, U.S.A.
Mor.	= Morelos, Mexico.
M.P.O.	= Military Post Office; Mobile Post Office (Canada).
Ms.	= Misiones, Argentina.
Mthe. et Melle.	= Meurthe-et-Moselle, France.
Mtzas.	= Matanzas, Cuba.
Mza.	= Mendoza Province, Argentina.
N.	= Neuquen, Argentina.
Nay.	= Nayarit, Mexico.
N.B.	= New Brunswick, Canada.
N.C.	= North Carolina, U.S.A.
N. Dak.	= North Dakota, U.S.A.
Nebr.	= Nebraska, U.S.A.
Nev.	= Nevada, U.S.A.
Newfd., Nfld.	= Newfoundland, Canada.
Nfk.	= Norfolk, England
N.H.	= New Hampshire, U.S.A.
N.J.	= New Jersey, U.S.A.
N.L.	= Nuevo Leon, Mexico.
N. Mex., N.M.	= New Mexico, U.S.A.
Northants., N'hants	= Northamptonshire, England.
Northd.	= Northumberland, England.

42

Notts.	=	Nottinghamshire, England.
N.S.	=	Nova Scotia, Canada.
N.S.W.	=	New South Wales, Australia.
N.T.	=	Northern Territory, Australia.
N.W.T.	=	Northwest Territories, Canada.
N.Z.	=	New Zealand.
O.	=	Ohio, U.S.A.
Oax.	=	Oaxaca, Mexico.
Okla.	=	Oklahoma, U.S.A.
Ont.	=	Ontario, Canada.
O.R.C.	=	Orange River Colony (obsolete)
Orte.	=	Oriente, Cuba.
Oreg.	=	Oregon, U.S.A.
Oxon.	=	Oxfordshire, England.
Pa.	=	Pennsylvania, U.S.A.
P. de C.	=	Pas-de-Calais, France.
P.E.I.	=	Prince Edward Island, Canada.
Pemb., Pembs.	=	Pembrokeshire, Wales
P.I.	=	Philippine Islands.
P.Q.	=	Province of Quebec, Canada.
P.R.	=	Puerto Rico
Pue.	=	Puebla, Mexico.
Punts.	=	Puntarenas, Costa Rica.
Pyr. Orles.	=	Pyrénées-Orientales, France.
Qld.	=	Queensland, Australia.
Qro.	=	Queretaro, Mexico.
Qroo.	=	Quintana Roo, Mexico.
Que.	=	Quebec.
R.A.A.F.P.O.	=	Royal Australian Air Force Post Office.
R.A.F.P.O.	=	Royal Air Force Post Office.
R.G. do Sul.	=	Rio Grande do Sul, Brazil.
R.I.	=	Rhode Island, U.S.A.
R.N.	=	Rio Negro, Argentina.
R.P.O.	=	Railway Post Office.
R.S.O.	=	Railway Sub (or Sorting) Office.
S.	=	Salta Province, Argentina.
S.A.	=	South Australia.
Sask.	=	Saskatchewan, Canada.
S.C.	=	South Carolina, U.S.A.; Santa Clara, Cuba; Santa Cruz, Argentina.
S.D., S. Dak., So. Dak.	=	South Dakota, U.S.A.
S.E.	=	Santiago del Estero Province, Argentina.
Seine Infre.	=	Seine Inférieure, France.
Seine Mme.	=	Seine Maritime, France.
S. et M.	=	Seine-et-Marne, France.

S. et O.	= Seine-et-Oise, France.
S.F.	= Santa Fé Province, Argentina.
Sfk.	= Suffolk, England.
Shrops., Salop.	= Shropshire, England.
Sin.	= Sinaloa, Mexico.
S.J.	= San Juan Province, Argentina; San José, Costa Rica.
S.L.	= San Luis Province, Argentine.
S.L.P.	= San Luis Potosi, Mexico.
S.O.	= Sorting Office.
Som., Somt.	= Somerset, England.
Son.	= Sonora, Mexico.
S.P.	= São Paulo, Brazil.
S.R.	= Southern Rhodesia.
Staffs.	= Staffordshire, England.
S.W.A.	= South West Africa.
Sy.	= Surrey, England.
T.	= Tucuman Province, Argentina.
Tab.	= Tabasco, Mexico.
Tam.	= Tamaulipas, Mexico.
Tas.	= Tasmania, Australia.
Tenn.	= Tennessee, U.S.A.
Tex.	= Texas, U.S.A.
T.F.	= Tierra del Fuego, Argentina.
Tlax.	= Tlaxcala, Mexico.
T.P.O.	= Travelling Post Office.
U.P.U.	= Universal Postal Union.
U.S.N.	= United States Navy.
U.S.S.	= United States Ship.
Va.	= Virginia, U.S.A.
Ver.	= Vera Cruz, Mexico.
V.I.	= Virgin Islands.
Vic.	= Victoria, Australia.
Vt.	= Vermont, U.S.A.
W.A.	= Western Australia.
Wash.	= Washington, U.S.A.
Westf.	= Westphalia, Germany.
Westmd.	= Westmorland, England.
W.I.	= West Indies.
Wilts.	= Wiltshire, England.
Wis.	= Wisconsin, U.S.A.
Wks., Warwks.	= Warwickshire, England.
Worcs.	= Worcestershire, England.
Württ.	= Württemberg, Germany.

W.Va.	= West Virginia, U.S.A.
Wyo.	= Wyoming, U.S.A.
Yorks., Yks.	= Yorkshire, England.
Y.T.	= Yukon Territory, Canada.
Yuc.	= Yucatan, Mexico.
Zac.	= Zacatecas, Mexico.

Aberdeen

Part of the attraction of the postmark collecting hobby is that there are so many attractive byways down which one may wander.

One such detour is that of attempting to gather from the world's far corners the 'date-stamp doubles' of well-known places, of which Aberdeen, Scotland's 'Silver City', is an interesting example.

In 1951 there were sixteen post offices bearing the name Aberdeen. In the directory of the world's post offices their names appeared in this order:

> Aberdeen, Cape Province, South Africa.
> Aberdeen, Idaho, U.S.A.
> Aberdeen, Kentucky, U.S.A.
> Aberdeen, Maryland, U.S.A.
> Aberdeen, Mississippi, U.S.A.
> Aberdeen, North Carolina, U.S.A.
> Aberdeen, Ohio, U.S.A.
> Aberdeen, South Dakota, U.S.A.
> Aberdeen, Washington, U.S.A.
> Aberdeen, New South Wales, Australia.
> Aberdeen, South Australia.
> Aberdeen, Nova Scotia, Canada.
> Aberdeen, Saskatchewan, Canada.
> Aberdeen, Scotland.
> Aberdeen, Jamaica.
> Aberdeen, Sierra Leone.

In the picture on page 45 you will see a pictorial record of one collector's attempt to 'capture' the postmarks of the world's postal Aberdeen's. At present this collector has thirteen postmarks from places named Aberdeen. No doubt some day his 'set' will be complete!

Accident

In Harry Graham's *Mr. Jones* these lighthearted lines occur:

> 'There's been an accident!' they said,
> 'Your servant's cut in half; he's dead!'
> 'Indeed!' said Mr. Jones, 'And please
> Send me the half that's got my keys.'

Something similar may have happened at Accident, Maryland, U.S.A.!

How, otherwise, could a place come to be so named?

That Accident exists we can discover from the map. A centre near which a state fish hatchery is established, it lies in the north-west corner of Garrett county, Maryland, near a union of the West Virginia-Maryland-Pennsylvania state lines.

Could it be that Accident was merely named – by accident?

Ace, King, Queen, Jack, Joker

It is easily possible for a date-stamp collector to 'hold all the Aces in the postmark pack'.

There is only one!

It is the name of a small community situated on State Highway 146, Polk County, Texas, U.S.A.

The other members of this postal version of the playing-card sequence are all located in the United States of America. King is in North Carolina, Queen is in Pennsylvania, Jack is in Missouri and Joker (whose post office no longer exists) is situated in the middle Atlantic state of West Virginia.

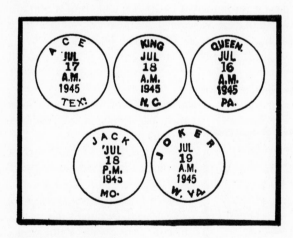

Aden (Number of Post Offices)

A colony and protectorate on the south coast of Arabia. In 1952 there were nine post offices in the territory.

Advertising

Among the odd uses to which, from time to time, postmarks have been put is that of advertising various goods and services.

Apart from the familiar use of meter marks by commercial concerns, and other users, there are many instances of the unconventional use of 'official' postal markings.

In 1924 a curious Italian pictorial slogan drew attention to the forthcoming publication of *Mata Hari*, 'a new romance by Guido da Verona'. Several years later, in 1959, mail deriving from an Australian exhibition held at Olympia, London, bore the cachet *A Town Like Alice* – the name of a novel by a contemporary best-selling novelist, Nevil Shute.

Another unusual use of the postmark as an advertising medium was the publication in an American trade paper of an announcement by the Grit Publishing Company, of Williamsport, Pennsylvania.

The advertisement contained the slogan 'GRIT SELLS SMALL TOWNERS'. Each word of the slogan was represented by a postmark, thus: Grit (Texas), Sells (Arizona), Small (Idaho), Towners (New York).

Ae

A village in the heart of the forest of Ae, Dumfries-shire, Scotland, which claims to possess the shortest name of any community in Britain.

The village was founded in 1949 when tenants of the first four houses to be completed were welcomed to their new homes by Sir Henry Beresford-Peirse, Director of Forestry in Scotland.

(See also Short Place Names in the alphabetical section of this book.)

Aero-Philatelic Exhibitions

Special postmarks have been in use from time to time in connection

with aero-philatelic exhibitions held in various parts of the world.

A special, winged postmark of this type was used for the Air Post ('Apex') Exhibition held in London, England, in 1934. A winged postmark on an official cover was also issued in connection with the Australian Air Mail Exhibition, held at Melbourne in October 1937, and a special postmark and cachet commemorated an Italian Air Exhibition and Congress in June 1939.

Air postmarks

In Great Britain air postmarks may be said to have had their beginnings with the inauguration of 'The First United Kingdom Aerial Post' in September 1911.

During the period 9th to 18th of that month letters and other postal packets were carried in a series of spectacular flights between Hendon and Windsor and special date-stamps, now of great rarity, were used to commemorate the occasion.

The wording on these postmarks was 'First United Kingdom Aerial Post' with the name of London or Windsor inserted according to the place of posting.

The flights were inaugurated by the then Postmaster-General in honour of the Coronation of Their Majesties King George V and Queen Mary and, in spite of adverse weather conditions, they made both aviation and postal history. On the inaugural flight from Hendon about 10,000 letters and newspapers were carried in a Bleriot monoplane which took ten minutes for the flight of 21 miles. 'This,' reported a contemporary newspaper, 'was accomplished in spite of a strong wind which only a score of months ago would have prevented all but the most reckless of aviators from attempting the journey. . . .'

Eight years later, in June 1919, the British naval airship R.34 commenced its historic flight across the Atlantic and on this occasion, also, a commemorative cancellation of the 'ring' type was used in which the letter and numerals 'R.34' were incorporated.

A more elaborate postmark bearing the words 'First Aerial Mail Great Britain to Australia' and the cachet 'Per Vickers Vimy Aeroplane to Australia' marked postal recognition of the pioneer flight of Captain Ross Smith in 1919–20.

More recent aerial date-stamps are no less significant in their portrayal of man's conquest of the air. The flights of Germany's Graf Zeppelin and the Schneider Trophy Races produced a number of interesting examples, as did the England-Australia Air Race and the Air Post Exhibition, London, in 1934. In April 1952 the inauguration of an air link between Great Britain and the faraway Falkland Islands was productive of a special commemorative postmark and when new services are opened up in all parts of the world the modern practice is almost invariably to perpetuate the event in postmark form.

Even packets carried on routine mail flights frequently have a story to tell for they often carry departure and arrival postmarks from which it is possible to calculate the time-table of air travel between distant parts of the world.

Associated with air postmarks are such aerodrome date-stamps as Shannon Airport (Eire), Gander Airport (Newfoundland), Croydon Airport, and innumerable examples from the service and civilian airport terminals and stations of overseas countries, including those of the Royal Air Force and the United States Army Air Force.

Alaska Dog Team Post
One mile north of the Arctic Circle, at Fort Yukon, Alaska, there is a log post office above the door of which hang a fine pair of moose antlers.

Fort Yukon, population 500, a metropolis in the bleak Arctic wilderness, is one of many similar trading posts which were dependent, until advances in air travel superseded them, on the Alaskan Dog Team Postal Services for the receipt and despatch of mail.

Here the climate runs to extremes. Fort Yukon has experienced Alaska's highest official temperature – 100 deg. Fahrenheit, as well as the new State's lowest – 78 degrees below zero. Here, gold was discovered in the 1850's and here trappers mush in their teams laden with pelts of mink, marten, ermine, fox, beaver and muskrat.

From this wilderness of Arctic space and silence comes the postmark reproduced below. It was imprinted on a letter carried by dog team post from Fort Yukon to Venetie.

Algeria (Number of Post Offices)
A country of North Africa organized in two divisions: Northern Algeria and Southern Territories.

In 1952 there were 815 post offices in Algeria.

All England Lawn Tennis Championships

A special postmark was in use at the All England Lawn Tennis Championship matches held at Wimbledon, London, S.W.19, in 1957.

All India Jamboree

A special pictorial postmark was in use for the All India Scout Jamboree held at Delhi in 1937.

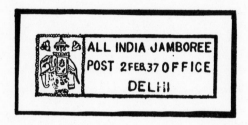

Alternative names

One result of wars and civil upheavals is that places change their names. In recent years, notably since 1919, many cities and towns throughout the world have become known by names other than those which may appear on older postmarks.

Again, some postal date-stamps may bear the local form of place-name which may differ from the long-accepted English language version. Thus Livorno (Italy) is more generally known to English-speaking people as Leghorn and Gand (Belgium) may be more familiar to us as Ghent.

Occasionally places may be renamed in order to avoid duplication or because the original name has been found to be undesirable or unacceptable to later generations.

To assist the collector to identify postmarks from places whose names have changed for these, and other, reasons here is a list of some altered or alternative postal place-names:

Former or National Name	Country	Alternative or Altered Name
Aalst	Belgium	Alost
Aberdeen	Australia	Burra North
Abo	Finland	Turku

51

Former or National Name	Country	Alternative or Altered Name
Adrianople	Turkey	Edirne
Agram	Jugoslavia	Zagreb
Aix-la-Chapelle	Germany	Aachen
Akkerman	U.S.S.R.	Belgorod Dnestrovski
Alchevsk	U.S.S.R.	Voroshilovsk
Aleksandropol	U.S.S.R.	Leninakan
Aleksandrovsk	U.S.S.R.	Zaporozhye
Alexandretta	Turkey	Iskenderon
Alger	Algeria	Algiers
Angora	Turkey	Ankara
Antioch	Turkey	Antakya
Antivari	Jugoslavia	Bar
Antwerpen (or Anvers)	Belgium	Antwerp
Arnswalde	Poland	Choszczno
Asterabad	Persia	Gurgan
Athenai	Greece	Athens
Ath Trasna	Eire	Newmarket
Aussig	Czechoslovakia	Usti
Bahia	Brazil	São Salvador
Baile Atha Cliath	Eire	Dublin
Bakhmut	U.S.S.R.	Artemovsk
Baltic Port	U.S.S.R.	Baltiski
Bartfa	Czechoslovakia	Bardijov
Basel	Switzerland	Basle
Batavia	Indonesia	Djakarta
Beograd	Jugoslavia	Belgrade
Beuthen	Poland	Bytom
Bjorneborg	Finland	Pori
Bobriki	U.S.S.R.	Stalinogorsk
Breslau	Poland	Wroclaw
Bromberg	Poland	Bydgoszcz
Brugge	Belgium	Bruges
Brunn	Czechoslovakia	Brno
Brusa	Turkey	Bursa
Brux	Czechoslovakia	Most
Bruxelles	Belgium	Brussels
Brzesc nad Bugiem	U.S.S.R.	Brest Litovsk
Bucuresti	Rumania	Bucharest
Cabhan	Eire	Cavan
Cattaro	Jugoslavia	Kotor
Ceara	Brazil	Fortaleza
Cernauti	U.S.S.R.	Czernowitz
Cetatea Alba	U.S.S.R.	Belgorod Dnestrovski
Chatalja	Turkey	Cataica

52

Former or National Name	Country	Alternative or Altered Name
Chisinau	U.S.S.R.	Kishinev
Coblence	Germany	Koblenz
Constantinople	Turkey	Istanbul
Corcaigh	Eire	Cork
Danzig	Poland	Gdansk
Demerara	Brit. Guiana	Georgetown
Den Haag	Netherlands	The Hague
Diarbekr	Turkey	Diyarbakir
Dirschau	Poland	Tczew
Dobrogea	Rumania	Dobruja
Dorpat	U.S.S.R.	Tartu
Dort	Netherlands	Dordrecht
Dulcigno	Jugoslavia	Ulcinj
Dunkerque	France	Dunkirk
Dushambo	U.S.S.R.	Stalinabad
Dvinsk	U.S.S.R.	Daugavpils
Edessa	Turkey	Urfa
Eger	Czechoslovakia	Cheb
Ekaterinburg	U.S.S.R.	Sverdlovsk
Ekaterinodar	U.S.S.R.	Krasnodar
Ekaterinoslav	U.S.S.R.	Dnepropetrovsk
Elista	U.S.S.R.	Stepnoy
Elsinore	Denmark	Helsingor
Enos	Turkey	Enez
Enzeli	Persia	Pahlevi
Eperjes	Czechoslovakia	Presov
Eszek	Jugoslavia	Osijek
Fellin	U.S.S.R.	Viljandi
Firenze	Italy	Florence
Fry	Arizona, U.S.A.	Sierra Vista
Funfkirchen	Hungary	Pecs
Gaillimh	Eire	Galway
Gallipoli	Turkey	Gelibolu
Gand	Belgium	Ghent
Ganja	U.S.S.R.	Kirovabad
Genève (or Genf)	Switzerland	Geneva
Genova	Italy	Genoa
Gensan	Korea	Wonsan
Gent	Belgium	Ghent
Gleiwitz	Poland	Gliwice
Gnesen	Poland	Gniezno
Goldingen	U.S.S.R.	Kuldiga

53

Former or National Name	Country	Alternative or Altered Name
Greytown	Nicaragua	San Juan del Norte
Guryev	U.S.S.R.	Chapayev
Heijo	Korea	Pyongyang
Helsingfors	Finland	Helsinki
Heraklion	Crete	Candia
Hindenburg	Poland	Zabrze
Hot Springs	New Mexico, U.S.A.	Truth Or Consequences
Hsinking	Manchuria	Changchun
Hutton Bushel	Yorks., England	Hutton Buscel
Iasi	Rumania	Jassy
Iglau	Czechoslovakia	Jihlava
Inbhear Mor	Eire	Arklow
Inis	Eire	Ennis
Insterburg	U.S.S.R.	Chernyakhovsky
Jakarta	Indonesia	Djakarta
Jakobstad	Finland	Pietasaari
Jakobstadt	U.S.S.R.	Jekabpils
Kaapstad	Union of S. Africa	Cape Town
Kamenskoe	U.S.S.R.	Dneprodzer-zhinsk
Karafuto	U.S.S.R.	Sakhalin
Karlovy Vary	Czechoslovakia	Carlsbad
Kepkypa (or Kerkyra)	Greece	Corfu
Khibinogorsk	U.S.S.R.	Kirovsk
Kingstown	Eire	Dun Laoghaire
Kjobenhavn	Denmark	Copenhagen
Klaipeda	U.S.S.R.	Memel
Koln	Germany	Cologne
Konisberg	U.S.S.R.	Kaliningrad
Konigshutte	Poland	Krowlewska Hutta
Kortrijk	Belgium	Courtrai
Kovno	U.S.S.R.	Kaunas
Kozlov	U.S.S.R.	Michurinsk
Kristiania	Norway	Oslo
Kuangchou	China	Canton
Kyongsong	Korea	Seoul
La Coruna	Spain	Corunna
Lagosta	Jugoslavia	Lastova
Laibach	Jugoslavia	Ljubljana
Leitmeritz	Czechoslovakia	Litomerice
Lemberg	U.S.S.R.	Lvov
Leuven	Belgium	Louvain

54

Former or National Name	Country	Alternative or Altered Name
Leva	Czechoslovakia	Levice
Libau	U.S.S.R.	Liepaja
Lisboa	Portugal	Lisbon
Livorno	Italy	Leghorn
Lugansk	U.S.S.R.	Voroshilovgrad
Luimneach	Eire	Limerick
Luzern	Switzerland	Lucerne
Magallanes	Chile	Punta Arenas
Mantova	Italy	Mantua
Maranhao	Brazil	São Luiz
Marburg	Jugoslavia	Maribor
Marienburg	Poland	Malbork
Marienske Lazne	Czechoslovakia	Marienbad
Mariupol	U.S.S.R.	Zhdanov
Mechelen (or Mechlin)	Belgium	Malines
Merv	U.S.S.R.	Mary
Milano	Italy	Milan
Minas	Uruguay	Lavelleja
Mitau	U.S.S.R.	Jelgava
Mohammerah	Persia	Khorramshahr
Monastir	Jugoslavia	Bitolj
Moskva	U.S.S.R.	Moscow
Moukden	Manchuria	Shenyang
Munchen	Germany	Munich
Munkacs	U.S.S.R.	Mukaceve
Napoli	Italy	Naples
Nikolaevsk	U.S.S.R.	Pugachev
Nikolsk-Ussuriisk	U.S.S.R.	Voroshilov
Nizhni Novgorod	U.S.S.R.	Gorki
Novo Nikolaevsk	U.S.S.R.	Novo Sibirsk
Olmutz	Czechoslovakia	Olomouc
Oos-Londen	Union of S. Africa	East London
Oostende	Belgium	Ostend
Oppeln	Poland	Opole
Ordzhonikidze	U.S.S.R.	Dzaudzhikau
Orenburg	U.S.S.R.	Chkalov
Padova	Italy	Padua
Papendorp	Union of S. Africa	Woodstock
Para	Brazil	Belem
Parahyba	Brazil	João Pessóa
Perm	U.S.S.R.	Molotov
Pernambuco	Brazil	Recife

55

Former or National Name	Country	Alternative or Altered Name
Pernau	U.S.S.R.	Parnu
Perovsk	U.S.S.R.	Kzyl Orda
Petrograd	U.S.S.R.	Leningrad
Petsamo	U.S.S.R.	Pechenga
Pilau	U.S.S.R.	Baltisk
Pishpek	U.S.S.R.	Frunze
Podgorica	Jugoslavia	Titograd
Pokrovsk	U.S.S.R.	Engels
Pola	Jugoslavia	Pula
Poltoratsk	U.S.S.R.	Ashkhabad
Porto	Portugal	Oporto
Port Petrovsk	U.S.S.R.	Makhach-Kala
Posen	Poland	Poznan
Pressburg	Czechoslovakia	Bratislava
Puerto Mexico	Mexico	Coatzacoalcos
Queenstown	Eire	Cobh
Ragusa	Jugoslavia	Dubrovnik
Rastyapino	U.S.S.R.	Dzerzhinsk
Ratibon	Poland	Raciborz
Ratisbon	Germany	Regensburg
Reichenberg	Czechoslovakia	Liberec
Revel	U.S.S.R.	Tallinn
Rodosto	Turkey	Tekirdag
Roma	Italy	Rome
Romanovski	U.S.S.R.	Kropotkin
Rybinsk	U.S.S.R.	Shcherbakov
St. Petersburg	U.S.S.R.	Leningrad
Salonika	Greece	Thessaloniki
Samara	U.S.S.R.	Kuibyshev
Samarkand	U.S.S.R.	Zarafshan
Sevilla	Spain	Seville
s'Gravenhage	Netherlands	The Hague
Shavli	U.S.S.R.	Siauliai
Simbirsk	U.S.S.R.	Ulyanovsk
Singora	Thailand	Songkla
Siracusa	Sicily	Syracuse
Sistova	Bulgaria	Svishtov
Smyrna	Turkey	Izmir
Sofiya	Bulgaria	Sofia
Sousse	Tunisia	Susa
Spoleto	Jugoslavia	Split
Stanislau	U.S.S.R.	Stanislawow
Stettin	Poland	Szczecin

Former or National Name	Country	Alternative or Altered Name
Stolp	Poland	Slupsk
Stavropol	U.S.S.R.	Voroshilovsk
Swinemunde	Poland	Swinoujscie
Tadmor	Syria	Palmyra
Tammerfors	Finland	Tampere
Tananarive	Madagascar	Antananarivo
Tanger	Morocco	Tangiers
Tavastehus	Finland	Hameenlinna
Teheran	Persia	Tehran
Teschen	Poland	Ciezyn
Tetschen	Czechoslovakia	Decin
Thorn	Poland	Torun
Tiflis	U.S.S.R.	Tbilisi
Tilsit	U.S.S.R.	Sovietsk
Torino	Italy	Turin
Trebizond	Turkey	Trabzon
Troppau	Czechoslovakia	Opava
Tsaritsin	U.S.S.R.	Stalingrad
Tver	U.S.S.R.	Kalinin
Uleaborg	Finland	Oulu
Usolye	U.S.S.R.	Berezniki
Varna	U.S.S.R.	Stalin
Venezia	Italy	Venice
Viipuri	U.S.S.R.	Viborg
Vlissingen	Netherlands	Flushing
Warszawa	Poland	Warsaw
Wien	Austria	Vienna
Wilno	U.S.S.R.	Vilna
Windau	U.S.S.R.	Ventspils
Xeres	Mexico	Jerez
Yuzovka	U.S.S.R.	Stalino
Zara	Jugoslavia	Zadar
Zaragoza	Spain	Saragossa
Zlin	Czechoslovakia	Gottwaldov
Zuider Zee	Netherlands	Ijsselmeer

Ampleforth College

Ampleforth College, Yorkshire – one of the few English schools to

possess its own postmark – is a monastic school with a Benedictine community attached to it.

The college (its motto is 'Dieu le Ward') stands beneath banks of trees overlooking the beautiful Vale of Pickering. In 1802 there were four pupils. Today there are over 600 in the public school and a further 100 in the preparatory school.

The post office, whose date-stamp is shown, was opened in 1913. It lies one mile to the west of the college.

Amundsen, Captain Roald

Norwegian explorer (1872–1928), who lost his life in the Arctic when going to the aid of the Nobile expedition.

A special postmark commemorated his death on Amundsen Mourning Day (14 December 1928).

Angela

Replying to a correspondent on 11 October 1958, the postmaster of Angela, Rosebud county, Montana, U.S.A., stated:

'The post office at Angela, Montana, has been in operation between forty and forty-five years. The present population of Angela is six.'

Anglo-Danish Festival

Conferences, exhibitions and festivals are often productive of interesting postmarks. Typical of these is the double-ring date-stamp reproduced below.

It was in use at the Anglo-Danish Festival held at Hull, Yorkshire, from 6-13 July 1957.

Angola (Number of Post Offices)
Portuguese possession in West Africa. Number of post offices (1952): 206.

Antigua (Number of Post Offices)
West Indies.

Part of a Federation within the British Commonwealth which came into existence on 3 January 1958. Post offices (including dependencies, Barbuda and Redonda): twelve.

Anzac Rifle Range
New South Wales, Australia.

This range was built during the First World War. The post office is open only seven days in each year to accommodate riflemen shooting in the New South Wales Rifle Association competitions. About 1,500 riflemen camp here.

The site is about twenty-two miles from Sydney.

Apt associations

Many postal place-names which might be commonplace on their own are apt and amusing when brought into association with other place-names in the pages of a collector's album.

Here is a brief list of such postmark place-names, to which the enterprising collector could add many more:

PEN (Bombay, India)	and INK (Arkansas, U.S.A.)
LONG (Somme, France)	and SHORT (Oklahoma, U.S.A.)
ROSE (Switzerland)	and THORN (Netherlands)
BACK (Sweden)	and FRONT (Italy)
OLD (England)	and NEW (W. Virginia, U.S.A.)
HIGH (Texas, U.S.A.)	and LOW (Quebec, Canada)
LOCK (Australia)	and KEY (W. Virginia, U.S.A.)
BACON (Philippines)	and EGG (Austria)
SALT (Spain)	and PEPPER (Jamaica)
GOOD (W. Va., U.S.A.)	and BAD (Bombay, India)
SAFE (Missouri, U.S.A.)	and SOUND (Cheshire, England)
GILBERT (Argentina)	and SULLIVAN (Wisconsin, U.S.A.)
BLACK (Alabama, U.S.A.)	and BLUE (Arizona, U.S.A.)
PAINS (Brazil)	and RELIEF (North Carolina, U.S.A.)
FAME (Oklahoma, U.S.A.)	and FORTUNE (Newfoundland, Canada)
THREE BROTHERS (U.S.A.)	and THREE SISTERS (Union of S. Africa)
LOVE (Canada)	and ROMANCE (Canada)
ALPHA (Australia)	and OMEGA (New Mexico, U.S.A.)
HURRY (Maryland, U.S.A.)	and SCURRY (Texas, U.S.A.)
HAMMER (Surrey, Eng.)	and TONGS (Kentucky, U.S.A.)
HONEYMOON (Canada)	and BRIDAL VEIL (Oregon, U.S.A.)
HAM (Somme, France)	and SANDWICH (Kent, England)
SUGAR (Idaho, U.S.A.)	and SPICE (W. Virginia, U.S.A.)
MAJOR (Brazil)	and MINOR (U.S.S.R.)

Argentina (Number of Post Offices)

In 1952 there were 5,169 post offices in the republic of Argentina.

Ark

A community in Gloucester county, Virginia, U.S.A.

The legend is that the first postmaster, William C. Trevilian.

submitted a list of 100 Biblical names to the United States postal authorities and asked them to select one by which the town should be known. They chose Ark.

The post office at Ark was established on 19 March 1886, and since then it has remained in the hands of the same family. Dates and details of Ark's postmasters and postmistresses are:

William C. Trevilian, appointed 19 March 1886.
Mary E. Trevilian, appointed 7 June 1907.
Edna E. Trevilian, appointed 11 April 1925.
Frederick H. Trevilian, appointed 31 August 1950.

Army postmarks

Army postal markings are a sphere from which much pleasure and interest may be derived. The collector's field ranges from the special cancellations of the Crimean War to the wide variety of marks used by the Army Field Post Offices of belligerent nations in the 1939–45 war. There are also many postmarks connected with wartime and peacetime camps and barracks, examples of which are Abbasia Barracks, Egypt, Catterick Camp, Blackdown Camp, Bulford Camp and Larkhill Camp. Other postal markings with a services association from stations in Britain or countries overseas are British Legion Village (Kent, England), Army H.Q. Simla, Military Dairy (Shadipur, India), and a special double-ring date-stamp used in connection with the British Military Mission to Ethiopia in 1949, as well as innumerable other postal markings deriving from campaigns and wars in bygone years.

Probably the first British service postmarks were those impressed on the letters of French prisoners in the war which raged intermittently with France from 1792 to 1815. The use of military postmarks continued in the Crimean War of 1854–56 when Army Post Offices were established at Balaclava, Constantinople and Scutari hospital. Items from this period are now becoming extremely rare, a valuation of £14, for example, being placed at a 1945 auction on a single envelope despatched in 1855 from one of the ships of Britain's Baltic Fleet.

Other campaigns from which have derived interesting postal material include the Persian War of 1856–57, the Zulu War of 1879,

61

the Sudan War of 1881–98, the South African War of 1899–1902, and
the Balkan Wars of 1912–13.

Atlas

A good atlas is an indispensable part of the postmark collector's
equipment. Not only does it add greatly to the enjoyment of the hobby
to discover on a map the place of origin of a postmark, a large-scale
atlas is also a source of much additional background information
including road and rail distances, contours and boundaries.

Apart from the familiar atlases, published in book form, it is quite
easily possible to obtain road maps and touring maps of almost every
region of the civilized world. Maps of this type can usually be obtained
on application to the tourist bureaux of the centres concerned, enclosing
appropriate postage or reply coupons where necessary.

Australia (Number of Post Offices)

Isaac Nichols was appointed Australia's first postmaster by a New
South Wales government order of 25 April 1809. The first Australian
post office was established at his office in Sydney and among other
duties he was required to board vessels in Sydney harbour to take
delivery of incoming mails. A commemorative postage stamp depicting
Mr. Nichols carrying out this duty was issued in April 1959.

In 1946 there were 8,114 post offices in the Commonwealth of
Australia. Figures issued by the Universal Postal Union in 1952
increased this figure to 8,315 made up as follows:

New South Wales	..	2,563
Queensland	..	1,297
South Australia ..	..	880
Tasmania	..	523
Victoria ..	..	2,414
Western Australia	..	638
		8,315

Australian National Antarctic Research Expedition

A special postmark bearing the words 'A. N. A. R. E., Macquarie Islands, Australia', was used in connection with the Australian National Antarctic Research Expedition of 1947.

Austria (Number of Post Offices)

The number of post offices in Austria is approximately 2,600. Postmarks – those of Vienna – were probably introduced about the year 1751.

Azemar postmarks

The name applied to an early type of machine cancellation in use in Britain from 1869 to 1872. The Azemar machine was devised by Mr. J. G. Azemar and was capable of postmarking letters at the then remarkable rate of nearly 50,000 letters an hour.

It produced an easily identifiable cancellation consisting of a circular date-stamp enclosing numerals and letters indicating the date and place of posting and a 7-barred 'canceller' in black.

B

Bad Heart

Some say Bad Heart (Alberta, Canada) took its name from the fight engendered by bad feeling, between Indians and whites on the banks of the near-by river.

There are others who say the name Bad Heart derives from the fact that many trees along the river bank have black centres.

Whichever version is right, and whichever may be wrong, the name Bad Heart makes an intriguing item in the files of a postmark collector!

Ball Ground

This is what Postmaster Guy D. McKinney had to say in reply to a request for information about how the small city of Ball Ground, Cherokee county, Georgia, U.S.A., acquired its name:

'. . . I take great pride in narrating to you the legend that has been handed down, from generation to generation, in regard to the naming of our fair city.

As the story goes a decisive "ball game" was once played here between two great Indian nations, the Creeks and the Cherokees, to decide the ownership of a tract of land that was in dispute between them. The game was similar to our baseball, though it differed in some respects.

As the legend goes the Cherokees won the game, were awarded the land, and remained in this part of the country until the last of the Indians were sent to the government reservations.

This is beautiful country; our city lies in a level valley between rolling hills. A good place to play a ball game: a good place to live. . . .'

Balmoral Castle
A British royal residence adjoining the River Dee, Aberdeenshire, Scotland.

The Balmoral Castle post office is open only when the Queen is in residence at the Castle. It deals only with the postal arrangements, both private and official, of Her Majesty's Household and staff.

'Barrel' post offices
Barrel post offices were unofficial ones set up by the sailors in clipper and whaling ship days. The sailors would rig up barrels or other containers and secure them to large rocks on remote islands in the middle of the ocean, and deposit their letters in the barrels. Other ships, passing by, picked up all the mail on their route and delivered it to the nearest regular post office.

A barrel post office of this type was said to be in existence at one time in the Straits of Magellan, opposite Tierra del Fuego. A contributor to *The Post Annual* in 1931 recorded having in his possession a post card mailed by a Captain Archer of the *Orellana* at this improbable 'post office' on 5 May 1901.

Battlefield

Battlefield, 3 miles north of Shrewsbury, Shropshire, takes its name from the Battle of Shrewsbury (1403) which took place here. In 1405 Henry IV built a church on the site of the battle.

Beauty

A small town (pop. 600) in Martin county, East Kentucky, U.S.A., in the Cumberland foothills.

It was formerly called Himlerville.

Belgian Congo (Number of Post Offices)

A colony of Central Africa ceded to Belgium in 1908.

In 1952 there were 194 post offices in the colony.

Belgium (Number of Post Offices)

In 1952 there were 1,956 post offices in Belgium.

Bermudas (Number of Post Offices)

British colony consisting of a group of about three hundred islands in the West Atlantic.

In 1952 there were thirteen post offices in the colony.

Bird In Hand

Bird In Hand, Lancaster county, Pennsylvania, U.S.A., took its name from an old hotel sign.

The sign pictured the proverb 'a bird in the hand is worth two in the bush' and portrayed a boy holding a bird in his hand and two birds in the bush beside him.

Bishop, Colonel Henry

Postmaster-General 1660–1663.

It was during Bishop's term of office that postmarks were introduced in England and postmarks of this type are known as 'Bishop Marks' to students of Postal History.

His appointment as a 'farmer' or contractor of the office of Postmaster-General was proclaimed on 16 January 1660, and he surrendered the grant on 6 April 1663.

Bishop lived at Henfield, in Sussex, where a memorial in the church wall recalls his connection with the postal service of seventeenth-century England. The parish register records that he was buried on 23 March 1692.

Bisley Camp
Woking, Surrey.

Bisley is a parish and village 3½ miles W.N.W. of Woking and 29 miles from London. The meeting of the National Rifle Association is held annually in July on Bisley Common.

In the summer of 1948 a special imprint was in use at Bisley Camp post office in connection with the shooting contests for the Olympic Games.

Boîte mobile
Under the provisions of the Anglo-French Postal Convention of 1843 the carriage of mail by private vessels equipped with a 'movable box (*boîte mobile*) was permitted.

A later Convention laid down special arrangements for the cancellation of letters carried in this way. The *boîte mobile* service was discontinued in 1939 and covers bearing such inscriptions as 'Southampton/France M.B.' are now comparatively rare.

'Bomba's postmark'
Sicily's first postage stamps were held up for years, before appearing in 1859, because Ferdinand II, king of the Two Sicilies, known as 'Bomba' for his practice of bombarding his rebellious subjects, felt the postmark might mar his classical features.

The king was finally persuaded to sanction a special postmark that cancelled only the frame of the stamp, leaving Ferdinand himself unblemished.

66

'Borderline cases'

An interesting postmark sideline is the gathering of items from communities along the frontier zones of neighbouring states.

In the United States of America, in particular, it is frequently the case that towns so situated take their names from the states whose borders they adjoin. Thus, Arkoma (Le Flore county, Oklahoma) is created from Arkansas and Oklahoma and Florala is a blend of Florida and Alabama on whose statelines it lies.

There are numerous other 'borderline cases'. Here is a list of some of them:

> Calexico (California–Mexico)
> Marydel (Maryland–Delaware)
> Texhoma (Texas–Oklahoma)
> Mexicali (Mexico–California)
> Monida (Montana–Idaho)
> Texline (Texas–New Mexico)
> Stateline (California)
> Texarkana (Texas–Arkansas)
> Kanorado (Kansas–Colorado)
> Kenvir (Kentucky–Virginia)

Botany

A suburb of Sydney, New South Wales, Australia, and probably the first settlement in Australia.

James Cook landed at Botany Bay about 1775. He gave it that name because of the variety of vegetation there. In 1787 Captain Phillip, with a shipload of convicts, also landed at Botany Bay but did not like the place and sailed on to Sydney.

Botany is 6½ miles from Sydney. Population: 29,500.

Box's Shop

An unusual Cornish postal place-name; near Launceston.

Boys Town

A village (pop, 1,000) in Douglas county, east Nebraska, U.S.A., near the Missouri River, 10 miles west of Omaha, developed from a refuge for homeless boys established by Father J. Flanagan in Omaha in 1917.

The village is located on 320 acres of farmland. It is supported by voluntary contributions and is governed by boys.

Brains

You need Brains to build a complete collection of modern French postmarks!

Brains is situated in the department of Loire Inférieure, western France.

British Antarctic Expedition

Behind a postmark bearing the words 'Brit. Antarctic Expd.' lies the story of Captain Scott's ill-fated South Polar Expedition.

When the *Terra Nova* left New Zealand for the Antarctic regions on 25 November 1910, she carried £100 worth of 1d. New Zealand postage stamps. These were used on letters posted via the *Terra Nova* to New Zealand and the outer world. For this purpose a post office was established by Captain Scott at Cape Evans.

The postmark illustrated is of particular interest for it bears the date on which news reached the expedition base of the deaths of Captain Scott and his gallant companions.

British Empire Exhibition, 1924–25

The British Empire Exhibition of 1924–25 was opened at Wembley Park by King George V on 23 April 1924. The exhibition cost many millions of pounds sterling to build and furnish and occupied 225 acres. Over 27,100,000 people attended it.

Several special postmarks and postal slogans were used in connection with the exhibition.

British Guiana (Number of Post Offices)
The only British colony on the mainland of South America.

First post office established by the Dutch at Demerara in 1783.

The colony joined the Universal Postal Union in 1877. In 1952 the number of post offices in British Guiana was 127.

British Honduras (Number of Post Offices)
British colony in Central America.

In 1952 there were thirty-two post offices in the territory.

First post office opened: 1857.

British Industries Fair
Special postmarks and postal slogans have been in use for several years in connection with the British Industries Fair held annually (with some exceptions) at Birmingham, England.

British Legion Village
Maidstone, Kent.

Behind this postmark lies the idealism of that modern Crusader, the late Field Marshal Earl Haig, who in 1921 founded the British Legion, an association open to ex-servicemen of all ranks.

The Legion represents some thousands

of cases in a year to the Ministry of Pensions. It has a housing scheme and a model village in Kent.

The village is entirely self-contained and includes a sanatorium with park grounds, shops, cottages and a post office whose imprint is illustrated on page 69.

British Postmark Society, The
The British Postmark Society was formed on 1 January 1958. Membership, originally seventeen, expanded quickly and reached fifty within four months of the founding of the society.

The aim of the society is to promote the study of modern British postmarks. A quarterly bulletin is issued and facilities for the exchange of postmark material are provided.

Annual subscription (1960) is 7s. 6d. per annum. Hon. Sec., G. R. Pearson, 42 Corrance Road, London, S.W.2.

Brumell, George
A well-known collector and authority on British postmarks and the author of several specialist books and articles on the subject.

A former secretary of the (British) Postmark Club, Mr. Brumell lived in Bournemouth, Hampshire. He died on 31 May 1950.

Brunei (Number of Post Offices)
A Protected State on the N.W. of Borneo, East Indies.

In 1952 there were six post offices in the territory.

Brunswick Star cancellation
An unusual type of postmark in use in Edinburgh, Scotland, for approximately ten years from 1863. It consisted of a circular date-stamp combined with a numbered obliterator containing the numerals '131' from which black lines radiated, giving a 'star' effect.

Brussels Fair
Several special types of official postmarks were in use at the Brussels Fair, Belgium, in 1958.

Brynteg
Anglesey, Wales.

Brynteg is an interesting example of a post office which takes its name from a *house* and not the village in which the post office is situated.

The name of the village in which Brynteg post office is established is Rhosfawr.

See also: Tynlon, Anglesey, Wales, and Tynygongl, Anglesey, Wales.

Buckingham Palace
The G.P.O.'s office in Buckingham Palace occupies almost half of the ground floor of the south wing and was reported, in 1951, to handle almost 2,000 letters a day.

The Palace was erected in 1703 on the site formerly occupied by Arlington House. It became a royal residence in 1761, when it was purchased by George III.

Bulgaria (Number of Post Offices)
No recent figures are available regarding the number of post offices in the republic of Bulgaria.

At 31 December 1940, the figure was 870.

Bumble Bee
Yavapai county, Arizona, U.S.A.

The legend is that in Arizona's pioneer days a troop of soldiers sent out to scout for Indians returned with the report that hostile Indians in the region were 'as thick as bumble bees'.

Butterfly postmarks
The description applied to a postmark of unusual design impressed on early issues of adhesive stamps in the state of Victoria, Australia.

Buxar Jail
A post office in Shahabad province, Bihar, India.

C

Cachet
The word *cachet* derives from the French, meaning a stamp or seal, and had its origin about 1639. Philatelically, it refers to a special hand- or machine-stamped mark or embellishment on a cover other than the conventional postmark or ordinary postal markings.

Modern cachets are often pictorial and frequently illustrate some commemorative aspect of the postage stamps, method of conveyance or place of origin of the cover on which they appear.

Cadillac post
A local delivery system of mail carriage by motor vehicle introduced in 1953 in certain regions of the United States.

Letters so carried bear a special cancellation reading: 'Cadillac Post: Local Route: Point of Mailing'.

Calgary Exhibition Post Office
Alberta, Canada.

A special post office, established in 1933, to provide postal facilities for working members and thousands of tourists who flock to Calgary's annual exhibition and 'Stampede'.

Located in Fort Calgary at the exhibition grounds, the Stampede post office is one of a kind. It combines a postal museum and a modern, efficient postal service in one small log building which is visited by upwards of 3,000 people a day during the six days annually on which the Stampede and exhibition are held.

The museum section of the office, in the lobby, contains specimens of original leather mailbags, photographs and drawings of early mail delivery systems and examples of early Canadian stamps.

An old shot-gun hangs in the post office and the cancelling board is part of a 220-year-old Douglas fir obtained from the Alberta Forestries Department.

Cambodia (Number of Post Offices)
A province of Indo-China under French Protectorate.

In 1952 there were seventy-five post offices in the province.

Canada (Number of Post Offices)
An independent member of the British Commonwealth.

In 1791 there were 11 post offices in Canada. By 1827 the number had risen to 101 and in 1858 there were 1,566.

Figures issued in 1947 gave the number of Canadian post offices as 12,033. By 1952 the number had increased to 12,644.

Cancellation
A philatelic term loosely, but often incorrectly, interchangeable with the word 'postmark'. Generally, the word cancellation refers to the defacing of adhesive postage stamps in such a way that after once being used they cannot be used again.

Cancelling ink
In Great Britain black ink consisting of carbon in oil is used for the cancellation of postage stamps where steel handstamps are used. For rubber stamps carbon in glycerine is used.

Cannon Ball
A community on the Cannon Ball River, Sioux county, North Dakota, U.S.A.

The town is named after the round, hard clay balls, a natural

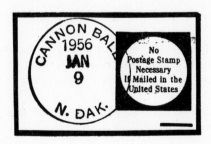

formation found in the area, about thirty inches in diameter, resembling cannon balls in appearance.

Cape Clear

Visitors to the small town of Cape Clear, Victoria, Australia, are always puzzled by its inappropriate name, for Cape Clear is situated about fifty miles west of Geelong – many miles from the sea.

Before it existed its site was a goldfield. Among the miners working there were two Irishmen, one of whom had the job of letting a bucket down a shaft by means of a windlass. He always gave the warning cry 'Kape clear!' as the bucket descended.

This call became so familiar in the area that the new town was named after it.

Capel Celyn

In the November 1958 issue of the *Post Office Magazine* this paragraph appeared above a photograph of Capel Celyn post office:

'Capel Celyn, Bala, Merioneth, is a village in the Tryweryn Valley which will be submerged because the valley is to be converted into a huge reservoir to supply Liverpool with water . . .'

Cape Nelson

Cape Nelson, Papua, British New Guinea, might be described as 'The Post Office That Never Was'.

In 1913 equipment (including a date-stamp) was forwarded to Cape Nelson by the government storekeeper but, apparently, official sanction for the opening of a post office there was subsequently withheld.

Ten years later the chief postmaster for the region wrote to the Resident Magistrate, Cape Nelson, as follows:

'It has been observed that you are using a post office date-stamp in your office for the cancellation of postage stamps.

As Cape Nelson is not a post office this practice is not in order and I would, therefore, request you to return the stamp to this office . '

The Resident Magistrate, Cape Nelson, despatched the date-stamp on 1 May 1923. But not before many postage stamps bearing the name of 'the-post-office-which-was-to-have-been' had found their way into the albums of collectors!

Cape Verde Islands (Number of Post Offices)
An overseas province of Portugal in the N. Atlantic.

Number of post offices (1952): thirty.

Cash
A small town (pop. 200) in Craighead county, Arkansas, U.S.A.

Originally called Soonover. Local opinion did not favour this name and when a post office was established the name was changed to Cash, after the Cache River, which is nearby. The main agricultural products of the region are cotton and rice.

Cerro de Pasco
Even the most ordinary-looking postmarks often have an entertaining background story.

On the face of it, the date-stamp of Cerro de Pasco seems commonplace enough. The pages of a gazetteer record the fact that it is a mining town of 19,000 people, on the Andean Highway, in the mountainous region of central Peru, South America.

What the gazetteer might not reveal is that Cerro de Pasco's post office has a unique claim to fame. Situated at an altitude of 14,385 feet (nearly 2¾ miles) Cerro de Pasco's post office is the highest permanent post office in the world. At this great height, so rarefied is the atmosphere, only Indians accustomed to the conditions can work for any length of time in the nearby mines.

75

Certificate of posting

In addition to the certificates which are issued by post offices in Great Britain in connection with the posting of *registered* packets, certificates are also issued in respect of unregistered mail.

A certificate for a letter is issued at a cost (1960) of one penny; for a parcel the certificate is issued without charge.

From the viewpoint of the postmark collector the value of such certificates lies in the fact that they contain a space for the date-stamp impression of the issuing office. They are therefore a convenient and inexpensive means of obtaining the postmarks of small rural offices and town sub-post offices which do not normally frank unregistered correspondence.

Ceylon (Number of Post Offices)

An independent member of the British Commonwealth of Nations.

In 1952 there were 1,298 post offices established in the island.

Chicago Railroad Fair

Special postmarks and commemorative covers were issued in connection with the Railroad Fair, an exhibition of ancient and modern railroad pageantry, held in Chicago, U.S.A., from 25 June to 2 October, 1949.

Chile (Number of Post Offices)

No recent details of the number of post offices in Chile are available.

In 1940 the number of post offices in this South American republic was 1,110.

76

China (Number of Post Offices)

No reliable figures are available of the number of post offices in the Chinese Republic.

The figure of 70,000 has been mentioned in reference books but the system of classifying post offices and postal agencies is different from that employed by most member-countries of the Universal Postal Union.

China's postal service was established in 1896.

Christkindl

The post office at Christkindl (Kristkindl = Christ Child) in Upper Austria does not look like a post office. It is situated in a small local inn belonging to the postal district of Unterhimmel and is open seasonally from 2 December to 6 January.

On an average 500,000 Christmas cards and Christmas letters from all over the world are handled here at Christmas time and such letters bear one of several types of special pictorial postmarks portraying the Infant Jesus. In December 1959 a postmark incorporating the music of "Stille Nacht, heilige Nacht" was in use at Christkindl.

Christmas

Christmas, Orange county, Florida, U.S.A., is a town where it is Christmas 365 days a year.

Established on Christmas Day, 1835, the site was then merely a log fort which had been successfully defended against the attacks of savage Seminole Indians. Created in a siege of war, the little community (population 250) is now dedicated to the cause of peace. A semi-official record of its 'industries' reads:

> 'Cattle-rearing, citrus groves, farming. Most important business: Worshipping God, promoting Love, Justice and Goodwill.'

The post office at Christmas was established on 27 June 1892, and now, each year, as 25 December approaches, about 300,000 separate pieces of mail are handled and franked with the postmark of Christmas in response to requests from all over the world.

Cinema
This curious name is borne by a small hamlet located in the Cariboo country of British Columbia, Canada.

Cinema was named by a certain Dr. Champlain who, more than forty years ago. decided the region could be made into a movie colony, and did much advertising with this object in view.

But nothing came of Dr. Champlain's project and today the main industries of the hamlet (population 250) are lumbering, mining and farming.

Cinema has a cinema show – three times a week!

Circle
A one-time gold-rush town of Alaska, U.S.A.

Its founders supposed the town to lie exactly on the Arctic Circle, hence the name. Actually, Circle lies about fifty miles south of the Arctic Circle.

Climax
Climax (population 860) in Lake county, Colorado, U.S.A., claims to have the highest all-the-year-round post office in the United States. It stands at an elevation of 11,320 feet and is situated near Mount Elbert, the highest point in Colorado (14,431 feet).

Clock Face
A district near St. Helens, Lancashire, England.

Closing postmark

A phrase often used by promoters of contests, etc., to indicate the final date by which entries can be entertained.

In competitions of this kind the postmark often plays an important part in deciding the validity, or otherwise, of last-minute entries.

Collector

A post office and centre of population in New South Wales, Australia.

Colonel Light Gardens

An unusual postal place-name deriving from the state of South Australia.

Colour postmarks

Postmarks are obtainable from various parts of the world of places bearing a wide range of 'colour' names.

Blue is in Arizona, Green in Kentucky; Brown and Pink can be found in West Virginia, Black in Missouri and Violet in Louisiana.

Not all the world's 'colour' names derive from the United States of America.

Indigo and Orange are Australian postal place-names and Gray can be found in France and Canada.

Oddly enough, throughout the world there appears to be no post office bearing the name Red.

Come By Chance

This pleasantly-named village is situated on Baradine Creek, 40 miles from Walgett, New South Wales, Australia. It consisted, in 1957, of five houses, a store, a post office and a school of art, and its population was then exactly twelve adults and four children.

The surrounding district is a wealthy w ool growing area.

79

Commonwealth Reply Coupons

Commonwealth Reply Coupons, valid for exchange between countries of the British Commonwealth, are obtainable from most post offices in Great Britain at a cost (1960) of 5d. each.

They are a useful means of pre-paying the reply postage on letters from correspondents in the British Commonwealth.

Cookhouse

One of South Africa's unusual postal place-names. It is a town of 2,000 people in Cape Province, on the Great Fish River, 85 miles north of Port Elizabeth. Wool, dairy-farming, stock-raising and fruit-growing are its principal industries.

Coronation

The story behind a postmark is not always apparent at first sight.

Coronation, in the province of Alberta, Canada, would probably consider itself to be an everyday town, and the gazetteer describes it prosaically enough: 'Population 633; 100 miles east of Red Deer. Grain elevators, dairying; in coal- and oil-bearing region . . .'

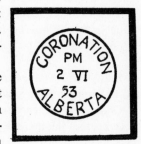

But on one date in recent history the name 'Coronation' had a special significance. That was the day on which, amid scenes of solemn grandeur, the Coronation took place in Westminster Abbey of Her Majesty Queen Elizabeth II.

And that is the date, 2 June 1953, borne by the postmark reproduced here.

Costa Rica (Number of Post Offices)

The collector of postmarks from Costa Rica, the Central American republic, has an interesting field to cover.

In 1945 there were 430 post offices in the republic.

Crash covers
A philatelic term used to describe postal matter salvaged from wrecked aircraft.

Crime detection
From the early period of their history postmarks have played an important part in the prevention and detection of crime.

Instances are recorded of savage sentences of up to seven years' deportation on the grounds of 'having defrauded the post office revenue by counterfeiting a frank' and in more recent times postal date-stamps have frequently featured in law suits and in criminal trials.

Cucumber
A postal place-name in McDowell county, West Virginia, U.S.A.

Cyprus (Number of Post Offices)
Mediterranean island administered by Great Britain.

In 1952 there were 706 post offices in the islands.

D

Dar-es-Salaam
The capital and chief seaport of Tanganyika Territory, East Africa. The name means 'haven of peace'.

Death Valley
An isolated region in Inyo county, California, U.S.A., near the Nevada border.

Decoy

A sub-post office of Newton Abbot, Devonshire, England.

Delville Wood

A post office in Natal, Union of South Africa, named after Delville Wood, France, where many South African troops fell during the battles on the Western Front in the First World War.

The title deeds of Delville Wood, France, are held by the Government of the Union of South Africa and, technically, Delville Wood in France is part of South Africa.

Denmark (Number of Post Offices)

In 1952 there were 1,636 post offices in Denmark.

The first Danish postage stamp was introduced on 1 April 1851 and each of the major postal offices was furnished with a handstamp for cancelling purposes.

Devils Slide

Devils Slide, Utah, U.S.A., owes its name to a curious geological formation consisting of two parallel limestone reefs which were left standing after the soft shale between had eroded in the course of centuries.

This formation lies in the mountains near the town of Devils Slide, a community of fifty homes in Morgan county.

Devils Tower

Devils Tower derives its name from an imposing 865-ft. tower of rock, formed perhaps 50 million years ago, in Crook county, which lies in the north-east corner of Wyoming, U.S.A.

The diameter of the base of the Tower is approximately 1,000 feet. At the top it averages 275 feet. The surface of the Tower covers about an acre and a half, upon which mosses, ferns, grasses, shrubs and sagebrush grow. Mice, pack rats and chipmunks have been seen there and the falcon and the hawk make it their home.

In 1906 the Tower was proclaimed a National Monument by President Theodore Roosevelt. The post office, and a museum, lie to the west of the Tower and nearby are camping grounds and picnic sites.

The fiftieth anniversary of the Tower's establishment as a National Monument was featured, in 1956, on a U.S. commemorative postage stamp.

Dictionnaire des Bureaux de Poste
A directory of the world's principal post offices compiled and issued, in two volumes, by the Universal Postal Union from its headquarters in Berne, Switzerland.

Difficult
No satisfactory explanation is offered for the name given to this village in Tennessee, U.S.A.

It lies near a creek at which a ferocious battle took place many years ago between Indians who were encamped there and a band of white settlers.

The post office at Difficult is no longer in existence.

Dime Box
Before there was a post office at Dime Box (Lee county, Texas, U.S.A.) the early settlers erected a community mail box on the trail to San Antonio. Passing freighters would then pick up the mail for a charge of one American dime for each round trip.

When petitions for a post office were

submitted to the United States postal administration a Dime Box resident, Dr. R. H. Womack, requested that if the post office were to be established its name should be Dime Box in order that the old community mail box should not be forgotten.

Direct Cable
Jamaica, British West Indies.
 The post office was opened on 1 July 1922 and closed on 31 October 1931.

D'lo

An amusing legend is associated with the naming of D'lo, a community in Simpson county, Mississippi, U.S.A.

 The story runs that when this section of the country was being mapped the surveyors found the region to be very low and swampy.

 A surveyor accordingly marked his provisional map 'Darned Low' but later thought better of this unconventional name and abbreviated the words to 'D'lo'.

Duplex mark

A term, somewhat loosely used by collectors, to describe an early type of British postmark consisting of a date-stamp adjoining a 'barred' obliterator which usually contained numerals to indicate the office of origin. In use approximately from 1844 to 1906.

Duplicates

There are many avenues for the exchange of postmark duplicates and it is always a good plan to have available as large a stock as possible for exchange purposes.

A convenient arrangement is to house one's duplicates in large envelopes, loosely classified in country or regional order according to the nature of the contents. Rare items or old covers should be kept 'entire'; other items should be trimmed to a standard 4″ × 2″ size for convenient handling.

Dutch Guiana (Number of Post Offices)

Overseas territory of the Netherlands in South America.

Number of post offices (1952): twenty-one.

Dutch John

An American postal place-name, in Utah. The post office at Dutch John was opened in 1958.

E

Easter postmarks

There are several place-names with an Easter association at some of which post offices are established.

Good Easter is the name of a parish 6 miles north-west of Chelmsford, Essex, England; Hen and Egg are respectively the names of post offices in Norway and Switzerland.

Easter Island, an overseas possession of Chile, lies in the Pacific Ocean.

85

Edith

This is what the postmaster of Edith, New South Wales, Australia, had to say, in January 1959, in reply to a correspondent's inquiry as to how the village got its name:

'The first families began to settle here about 120 years ago but it was not declared a village until the early 1880s. Our village was called Edith after Edith Bailey who was the oldest girl at school at the time. This lady, now Mrs. Edith Kissell and 88 years of age, is living at Gunning, New South Wales.

The district is completely rural, and farming (mainly peas and potatoes and the grazing of sheep and cattle) is carried on extensively in this tableland region.

As the altitude ranges between 3,900 and 4,300 ft. the climate is cold in winter, with some snow, and has a very mild summer. Willows and poplars and Kentish cherries, gooseberries, raspberries and currants are grown at most homes and bulbs like tulips and daffodils do very well . . .'

Egypt (Number of Post Offices)

From 1 February 1958 (with Syria) a member State of the United Arab Republic.

In 1952 the number of post offices in Egypt was 1,425.

Eighty Eight

Here is a postmark with an entertaining tale to tell!

The story runs that when the establishment of a post office was planned at this little community, in Barren county, Kentucky, U.S.A., it was discovered that the elderly man elected as postmaster could neither read nor write.

Then someone had an idea.

'Call the place 88,' he suggested, 'anyone can read and write *that* name!'

So runs the legend.

But Duie C. Sikes, postmaster here in 1956, had another theory.

'Our town,' he said, 'is exactly 8.8 miles from Glasgow, the nearest big city. I reckon *that's* how Eighty Eight got its name.'

Eire (Number of Post Offices)

Formerly Irish Free State; attained complete independence 1937.

In 1951 there were 2,309 post offices in the republic.

England

England, Arkansas, U.S.A., is a town of 3,000 people, 25 miles south-east of Little Rock. It lies in a rich farming area (cotton and rice) on land believed to have been, at one time, part of the Gulf of Mexico.

The town is named after an early settler named England.

Enid

There is an interesting legend concerning the way in which Enid, now a thriving city of 36,000 people in Garfield county, Oklahoma, came to be so named.

According to the story two strangers were eating here in the pioneer days and one asked his companion the name of the place.

The other man looked up and said, 'I reckon it's called Enid.'

He had looked at the word 'Dine' written on the window of the eating-place and had mis-read the reversed lettering.

Somehow the name stuck to the locality and it has remained 'Enid' ever since.

Entire

A philatelic term used by collectors to signify an envelope, wrapper, letter, etc., in the condition as carried postally.

Envelopes

As wrappers for enclosing letters envelopes were not in ordinary use in Britain until after the introduction of the Penny Postage system in 1840.

They were known in France, however, in the seventeenth century.

See: Mulready envelope.

Errors

The mis-spelling of place-names, and other postmark errors, occur more frequently than one might expect.

Date-stamp specimens of *St. Noets*, so spelt, had a prideful place in the files of a Hampshire collector although modern works of reference give the spelling of this Huntingdonshire market town as St. Neots. Holkham village, in Norfolk, England, has been known to employ a date-stamp in which the second aspirate had been unaccountably dropped, and some years ago Paignton, Devon, caused joy among collectors and consternation among postal officials by appearing as *Paington* in postmark form.

North Broomhill (Morpeth, Northumberland) has been recorded as appearing with a missing 'H' and Ryde, in date-stamp guise, has been erroneously associated with the Isle of *Whit*. Singapore, similarly ill-treated, was once postally rechristened *Snigapore* and Llanarth's industrious population was once located, by a postmark oversight, in the make-believe county of *Cardingshire*.

On yet another occasion Braes-River, a Jamaican place-mark, mysteriously took the form of *Braze-River*; Whittlesey (Peterborough, England) has appeared in that form and (in 1907) in the form of *Whittlesea*; Kuwatt has appeared in that guise and as *Kuwait* and *Emborrow* (Bath, Somerset, England) is now Emborough in the official list of United Kingdom post offices.

In 1948 Athabaska (Alberta, Canada) date-stamped correspondence with the name so spelt. By November 1950, a change of heart, or at least a change of spelling, had occurred. Athabaska had become Athabasca. Smith Falls – or Smiths Falls, or Smith's Falls (Ontario, Canada) – underwent even more harrowing changes at the hands of postal officials. In 1937 the postmark said 'Smith's Falls'. In February 1950 the name had become 'Smith Falls' but in December 1950, a further change had occurred. 'Smith Falls' again became 'Smiths Falls' – but this time without the apostrophe.

There are many other instances of postal mis-spellings or variations. Officially Kirkbymoorside (Yorkshire, England) is rendered in this way – a derivation from 'Kirk-by-the-Moorside'. Postally, however, it still appears as Kirby Moorside.

On 2 January 1958 Assawoman, a curiously-named town in Virginia, U.S.A., was using a double-ring date-stamp with the name spelt as quoted here. The following day a single-ring date-stamp was in use and this time the name took the form of 'Asawoman'.

The modern spelling of place-names is often different from that found on old letters and this fact accounts for apparent discrepancies on correspondence of the eighteenth and nineteenth centuries. Thus,

Aylesbury (Buckinghamshire, England) was '*Aylsbury*' in 1842, although the spelling on earlier postmarks conformed to that of the present day. Occasionally correspondents and residents in town would be at variance with the postal authorities on the subject of how a place-name should be rendered. Thus, a correspondent in 1806 might style Rugely (Staffordshire) in that form while the postmark on the letter would read '*Rudgeley*'.

Occasionally one mistake can lead to another. During the year 1918 letters passing through the village of Helhoughton, West Norfolk, bore the date-stamp *Elhoughton*. From letters in the possession of collectors it is evident that the error escaped unnoticed for some considerable time By October, 1918, however, the mystery of the missing "H" had clearly been solved in official quarters and the letter was reinstated in its rightful place.

In Helhoughton, alas, the rejoicing was short-lived.

Date-stamp impressions bearing the date 7 October 1918 and the spelling *Helhaughton* are still treasured by collectors!

Such happenings, though rare, are by no means unique. Date-stamp imprints have been known where the place-names have been inverted, reversed and even omitted. On one occasion the last two numerals of the year 1899 were inserted upside down, so that a number of astonished addressees received correspondence that had, apparently, been thirty-three years in transit; other dating errors include the incorrect use of numerals whereby February acquires thirty days, November thirty-one days and, as illustrated, December is credited with at least sixty-one days!

Evening Shade
The town of Evening Shade, Sharp county, Arkansas, U.S.A., lies in a narrow valley surrounded by high hills. In the early days of the town these hills were covered with tall virgin pine which shaded the valley early in the afternoon – and gave the town its name.

Exhibitions and conferences

During the past 100 years many important functions of a local, national or international character have been postally honoured with commemorative date-stamps covering a wide variety of activities ranging from naval conferences and philatelic exhibitions to sanitary congresses and dog shows.

In England the pioneer of special exhibition postmarks was the specimen introduced for use at the Great Exhibition of 1851. Opened by Queen Victoria on 1 May that year, the Great Exhibition was a memorable forerunner of many that were to follow. The Exhibition grounds, in Hyde Park, London, covered 21 acres in which the displays of nearly 14,000 exhibitors were seen by six million people before the Exhibition closed in October.

With receipts totalling over £500,000 the Great Exhibition set the seal of success upon displays of this nature and in 1862 a second great exhibition was held in South Kensington. For this, also, a special postal date-stamp was brought into use.

Thereafter, in slightly less than thirty years, at least nine major exhibitions were held in places as widely separated as Paris, Philadelphia, Vienna, Melbourne and Sydney.

London was again the venue when, in 1887, the American Exhibition took place and for this, as for the Penny Postage Jubilee celebrations at the Guildhall and South Kensington three years later, the honour of a special postal imprint was conferred.

From that time forward exhibition and conference postmarks appeared to be granted formal status as a postal feature of any great foregathering. The Royal Naval Exhibition of 1891 and the Cork International Exhibition of 1902 were duly commemorated, while the Franco-British Exhibition of 1908, which was attended by more than 8,000,000 people, was similarly productive of date-stamps which, today have a rising value. In 1894 the great Agricultural Show of the Royal Agricultural Society of Great Britain took place at Cambridge. For this, and for succeeding shows at Reading, Bournemouth, Portsmouth and Wolverhampton, various types of interesting date-stamps were in use.

The sombre European war clouds overhung the International Exhibition of Bristol, in 1914, and from that date, for nearly a decade, the issue of commemorative date-stamps would appear to have lapsed until the holding of an International Stamp Exhibition in London in 1923.

The British Empire Exhibition of 1924–25 brought about a great revival in this field and was productive of several distinctive types of postal impressions.

The interval of comparative peace between the two World Wars produced a wealth of intriguing material for the albums of the collector. In 1926 a large exhibition was held at Shepherd's Bush, London, and in 1928 philatelists flocked to the London Stamp Exhibition. Two years later the representatives of the world's great naval Powers were gathered in London for the Naval Conference and, in the same year, were held the Socialist Esperanto Conference and the Monetary and Economic Conference.

These meetings, otherwise unconnected, possessed from the viewpoint of the postmark collector one point of parallel interest: they were all considered by the postal authorities to be of sufficient importance to merit the use of special postal facilities and cancellation marks.

Thereafter the list is legion and is virtually world-wide. Scotland offers the date-stamps of the Glasgow Empire Exhibition of 1938 and of successive Royal Highland Shows for which special imprints were in use. The United States, to select two random examples from the wealth of material available, postally honoured the New York World's Fair of 1939 and the Chicago Railroad Fair ten years later. In Berlin the occasion of the 11th Olympiad of the Olympic Games produced a swastika-decorated memento, and in Egypt a bi-lingual cancellation marked the opening, in 1947, of the 36th Interparliamentary Union Conference. Complementary to these are the outpourings of France (International Aerial Post Exhibition, 1930), South Africa (National Philatelic Exhibition, Port Elizabeth, 1956), Switzerland (International Printing Exhibition, Lausanne, 1957), and Belgium (the Brussels Fair, 1958) as well as innumerable other examples from these and other parts of the world.

The specialist in exhibition and kindred types of cancellations has an extensive range from which to select his material. It is also one which fully rewards, in interest and visual appeal, the long search which may sometimes precede the thrill of discovering a coveted specimen.

F

Fairplay
The county seat of Park county, central Colorado, U.S.A., in the Rocky

Mountains, on the South Platte River. Population 500; altitude: 9,964 feet. The main industries of the region are mining, hay, and stock raising.

Originally a mining camp, Fairplay is said to have derived its name from the fact that when gold was discovered in the district prospectors were lined up and were run off at the start of a gun to ensure that all received 'fair play' in establishing their claims.

Fairy
The town of Fairy, Texas, U.S.A., was originally known as Martin's Gap after a settler who was killed by the Indians and buried in a gap in the mountains.

When a post office was established here in the 1850's the citizens of Martin's Gap asked the United States postal authorities if the name of the town could be changed to Fairy in honour of a popular little midget woman, the daughter of a Confederate captain who had settled the community.

Faith, Hope, and Charity
In the postmark sense Faith can be found in North Carolina and South

Dakota (U.S.A.), Hope in Devonshire (England) and in Denbighshire (Wales), and Charity, now obsolete, was the name of a post office in Missouri (U.S.A.).

Falkland Islands (Number of Post Offices)
A British Crown colony in the South Atlantic.

Two permanent post offices are established in the colony, namely, Port Stanley and Fox Bay, and additional post offices are established at the colony's dependencies which include South Georgia, Graham Land, South Shetlands and South Orkneys.

Famous names

It is possible to accumulate a considerable collection of postmarks in which the names of well-known people are incorporated.

Examples of this are:

Gene Autry
A post office in Carter county, Oklahoma, U.S.A.

Robin Hood
The name of a district and post office near Wakefield, Yorkshire, England.

Kit Carson
A postal place-name in Cheyenne county, Colorado, U.S.A.

Davy Crockett
A sub-post office station of Greeneville, Tennessee, U.S.A.

The names of George Washington, Adolf Hitler and many other famous and infamous people have also been commemorated in postmark form.

Famous postmark collections

During recent decades many large and celebrated collections have been gathered by specialist collectors in various fields of the postmark hobby.

The name of the late Mr. C. F. Dendy Marshall is outstanding among British specialists as he was among the first to realize the immense field of interest which lay in the acquisition and study of material relating to the British Post Office.

Among contemporaries of Mr. Dendy Marshall, whose researches and writings added much to the scope and interest of the postmark subject, were the late Mr. J. H. Daniels, of Brighton, and the late Mr. George Brumell, of Bournemouth, a former honorary secretary of the Postmark Club. During their life-time both these collectors amassed large and valuable selections of carefully catalogued postmark material.

In the United States of America many very large collections have been gathered by postmark enthusiasts. In January 1958 the collection of Mr. Anthony J. Horner, of Franklin, Minnesota, consisted of 76,500 items. Another American collector, Mr. E. C. Schallis, of East Orange, New Jersey, had, by 1954, harvested a range of over 60,000 postmarks of cities, towns and communities in the United States during his thirty years as a date-stamp enthusiast.

In 1949 Mrs. H. F. Simons, an American woman of Willoughby, Ohio, had a collection of 30,000 postmarks, gathered in twelve years. On one occasion Mrs. Simons contrived a 1,000-word short story using only postmarks as her means of narration.

Festival of Britain
Special postmarks were in use in connection with the Festival of Britain, in 1951.

The millionth visitor to the Festival arrived three weeks after the opening day (4 May) and the total attendance was 8,455,863.

5th Clause Posts
So called from the Clause of the Act of Parliament, of 1801, which enabled the Postmaster-General to undertake the conveyance of correspondence to the inhabitants of towns and villages which had no post offices, at rates agreeable to the Postmaster-General and the users of the service.

Special postal markings were used in conjunction with this facility. They are to be found on old letters in many varied forms but usually consisted of a mark incorporating the name of the post town and various renderings of the words '5th Clause Posts'.

The use of these postal markings virtually ceased with the introduction of Uniform Penny Postage in 1840.

Fiftysix
Fiftysix, Stone county, Arkansas, U.S.A., takes its name from the number of the school district in which it is situated.

It is one of many places whose names consist of numbers.

See: Numeral postmarks.

94

Figtree

A community south-east of Bulawayo, Southern Rhodesia; altitude 4,522 feet.

It is here, prior to 1890, that traders and hunters were detained until permission to proceed had been obtained from the Matabele king.

The wild figtree at which they waited is a well-known landmark and from it Figtree derives its name.

Fiji (Number of Post Offices)

A colony of the western Pacific, comprising a group of 322 islands of which 106 are inhabited.

Post offices in the colony (1952): ninety-eight.

Finland (Number of Post Offices)

A republic of N. Europe. Independent state since 1917.

According to figures issued by the Universal Postal Union the number of post offices in Finland in 1952 was 4,169.

First Day Cover

A complete envelope, often specially printed with commemorative details, generally used in connection with the first day of issue of new issues of adhesive postage stamps.

In more general terms, first day covers may be used in connection with certain important non-philatelic events and national occasions. In this sense they would more accurately be described as commemorative covers.

First Day postmark

A postmark bearing the date on which the office of origin was first opened; alternatively, a postmark bearing the date on which the name of the office of origin was changed.

Examples of both types are shown below. The postmark of Ireland Wood, Leeds (Yorkshire, England), bears the date – 4 February 1952 – on which this sub-post office was opened.

The postmark of Sierra Vista (Arizona, U.S.A.) bears the date – 20 October 1956 – on which the name of this town was changed from Fry, by which name it was formerly known.

First postal place-name (Great Britain)

Alphabetically speaking, the first postal place-name in Britain is Abberley, Worcestershire, a parish 4 miles south-west of Stourport.

First United Kingdom Aerial Post

An official service was inaugurated between Hendon and Windsor in September 1911, to commemorate the Coronation of Their Majesties King George V and Queen Mary.

A famous aviator of the period, Gustav Hamel, set off on the pioneer flight with 23 lb. of letters, etc., including some addressed to King George V and the Royal Household at Windsor. The flight took 10 minutes. Altogether, about

1,000 lb. of mail was carried during the short period (9–18 September) of the operation of this service.

(See also Air Postmarks).

Floating post offices

In British Columbia, Canada, a store and post office building erected on a raft of large cedar trees wired together has been located in Simoon Sound, 160 miles north of Vancouver, since about 1910. Another floating post office in British Columbia is established on the cruise ship *Scenic* which runs on a daily schedule in spring and summer from Vancouver to Wigwam Inn, a distance of 22 miles. The *Scenic* is the official government post office for the region and uses the postmark Burrard Inlet.

A floating post office service was opened at Detroit, U.S.A., on the Detroit River, in April 1946, a 65-ft. steel motor craft being used for the delivery of mail to steamers plying the Great Lakes.

See also: Lake Winnipesaukee R.P.O. and Naval Cancellations.

Floral postmarks

Floral postmarks have been issued on a number of occasions.

Examples of their use are:

> The Hague Flower Show (Netherlands) April 1939.
> Essen Garden Exhibition (Germany) April 1938.
> Berne Flower Show (Switzerland) June 1937.
> Boskoop Flower Show (Netherlands) April 1937
> Dresden Horticultural Exhibition (Germany) August 1936.
> Chelsea Flower Show, May 1953.

There are also innumerable instances of floral place-names in postmark form, e.g. Carnation (Washington, U.S.A.), Lobelia (W. Virginia, U.S.A.), Lupin (China), Marguerite (British Columbia, Canada), Rose (Great Britain, Italy, U.S.A., etc.), Scilla (Italy) and Tulip (Ohio, U.S.A.).

Fort Chimo

A seaport and air base, Province of Quebec, Canada.

Fort Chimo was established as a fur trading post by the Hudson's Bay Company in 1830.

Forty Foot
A sub-post office and locality in Bridlington, Yorkshire, England.

Four by two
Four inches by two inches is the size to which many collectors of modern postal date-stamps prefer to trim their postmarks after removing them from the envelope, post card, etc., on which they were imprinted.

This size is the one most generally adopted by collectors in the U.S.A.

Postal markings should never be removed from a first day cover or a cover likely to be of historical interest, nor should they be removed when their interest is linked with other markings which may appear on the cover.

Four Mile Bridge
Holyhead, Anglesey, Wales.
This village is on Holyhead Island, four miles from Holyhead.

Foxholes
A village and post office in the Yorkshire Wolds, East Riding, north-east England, near Driffield.

France (Number of Post Offices)
Figures issued in 1927 gave the number of post offices in France as 16,462.

By 1952 this number had increased to 19,890.

The use of postmarks in France began about the year 1695.

Franco-British Exhibition
A special postmark was in use at the Franco-British Exhibition which was held in London in 1908 and attended by over 8,000,000 people.

Freak postmarks
Local conditions, an imperfect 'strike' from the postmaster's handstamp, even urgent exigencies may account for a number of postmark 'freaks'.

There may, it is as well to remember, be a typhoon blowing outside the post office or a revolution taking place in the piazza a quarter of a mile away. Amid such distractions the local postmaster might be forgiven if he overlooked the fact that September has only thirty days or that the letter 's' from the date-stamp type-holder has slipped through a crack in the post office floorboards.

So it is that postmark freaks, though rare, sometimes come within the collector's reach. One such freak was referred to, in 1956, in a London newspaper. An illustration depicted a postmark bearing the name Widnes, Cheshire. Postally, and geographically, Widnes is in Lancashire. The apparent error was, in fact, due to part of the postmark of Crewe, Cheshire, having been superimposed upon part of the postmark of Widnes, Lancashire.

See also: Errors.

Freedom
A town in Carroll county, New Hampshire, U.S.A., on a quiet road near the state's union with Maine.

The town celebrated its 125th anniversary in 1957 and each year on America's Independence Day, the Fourth of July, its postmistress is inundated with requests from patriotic Americans for postmarks of the town.

Freezywater
A hamlet and sub-post office 2 miles north-east of Enfield, Middlesex, England.

French Cameroons (Number of Post Offices)
A self-governing Trust territory of West Africa.
  Number of post offices (1952): seventy-six.

French Equatorial Africa (Number of Post Offices)
An overseas territory comprising the French-controlled colonies of Gaboon, Middle Congo, Ubangi-Chari and Chad in Central Africa.
  There were 125 post offices in the region in 1952.

French Fair (Melbourne, Australia)
This is one of many interesting Australian postmarks.
  The date-stamp incorporates a cock, the symbol of France. It was applied to mail posted at a French trade fair held in Melbourne, Australia, in 1958.

French Oceania (Number of Post Offices)
French overseas territory in the eastern Pacific.
  Post offices in the territory numbered thirty-two in 1952.

French Somaliland (Number of Post Offices)
French overseas territory of East Africa.
  Number of post offices (1952): five.

French West Africa (Number of Post Offices)
A consolidation of eight French colonies: Senegal, Guinea, Ivory Coast, Upper Volta, Dahomey, French Sudan, Mauritania, and Niger.
In 1952 there were approximately 350 post offices in the territory.

G

Gazetteer
Part of the entertainment and interest of the postmark hobby is the desire it evokes to know more about people and places. For this purpose a good gazetteer is an essential piece of equipment.

By means of it, interesting background facts can be obtained regarding the places from which one's date-stamps derive. Details of some well-known gazetteers are included in the bibliography at the end of this book.

It may be useful, however, to compile and keep up to date a virtual gazetteer of one's own by noting interesting geographical facts from books, newspapers and magazines and recording them on the filing cards or albums in which one's postmark collection is housed.

German Federal Republic (Number of Post Offices)
In 1952 the number of post offices in the German Federal Republic (West Germany) was 25,942.

No figures are available for the area controlled by the Soviet Union.

Ghana (Number of Post Offices)
On the Gulf of Guinea, West Africa.

An independent dominion in the British Commonwealth. Formerly called the Gold Coast, the dominion came into existence on 6 March 1957, when the four component parts, the Colony, Ashanti, the Northern Territories and Togoland, under United Kingdom Trusteeship, achieved independence under a parliamentary system of government.

In 1952 there were 460 post offices in the Gold Coast territory as it then existed.

Giant's Causeway

A famous natural formation of basaltic columns on a promontory of the north coast of Ireland, in County Antrim.

The postmark of Giant's Causeway reads: 'Giant's Causeway, Bushmills, Co. Antrim.'

Gibraltar (Number of Post Offices)

British colony comprising a narrow peninsula on the S.W. coast of Spain.

Number of post offices (1952): three.

Gilbert and Ellice Islands (Number of Post Offices)

A colony consisting of thirty-seven islands in the Pacific, spanning about two million square miles of ocean. The colony includes Ocean, Christmas, Fanning and Washington Islands.

There were thirty-two post offices in the colony in 1952.

Go Home

A somewhat inhospitably named summer season post office in the province of Ontario, Canada.

Golden Temple

An interesting postal marking from India is that of the Golden Temple, Amritsar. The temple from which the post office derives its name was built of marble, copper and gold-leaf at fabulous cost to house *Granth Sahib*, the sacred book of the Sikhs.

Golden Valley

A village and post office, Cape Province, South Africa. It is the centre of the apricot industry of this region.

Goodluck

The name of a post office formerly established in Kentucky, U.S.A. It was closed some years ago.

Goodnight (New South Wales, Australia)

In the early days when paddle steamers plied the Murray, Australia's principal river, an old shepherd lived by himself near a bend on the river, about 20 miles north-west of Swan Hill (Victoria). It was a lonely existence with only his dogs and the flock of sheep for company.

The old man's only contact with the outside world was the passing paddle boats He would stand on the water's edge as they chugged past, calling out a cheery 'Goodnight'.

The steamermen started to look out for him. 'Soon be reaching old Goodnight,' they would say as they approached the river bend.

The name persisted when the area was opened up and now it is officially the name of the little settlement that has developed and, as you see, the postmark bears this name.

Goodnight (Texas, U.S.A.)

Goodnight, Texas, has a less romantic explanation of its unusual name than one might expect.

This Texan town, in Armstrong county, derives its name from Colonel Charles Goodnight, who established the first ranch in the 'Panhandle' of Texas in 1872.

Graf Zeppelin

The postal marking illustrated is one of many used during the German Graf Zeppelin's nine years of active service, during which over 500 flights were made and nearly 18,000 passengers carried.

Completed in 1928 and registered as 'LZ – 127' the Graf Zeppelin flew mail, freight and passengers a total distance of 1,028,793 miles and crossed the Atlantic 139 times.

Her round-the-world flight in 1929,

under the command of Dr. Hugo von Eckener was accomplished with only three intermediate stops in 20 days and 4 hours.

The accompanying postmark was inscribed on a post card addressed to 'Major Freiherr v. Wangenheim, of Lubeck' and is one of a series of propaganda cachets in support of the 'deliverance' of Sudetenland.

Greece (Number of Post Offices)
According to statistics issued by the Universal Postal Union there were 1,498 post offices in Greece in 1952.

Guatemala
The most northerly of the Republican States of Central America.

Postmarks were probably introduced in this republic in 1871. In 1894 there were 186 post offices.

H

Ha! Ha! Bay Junction
The name of a post office formerly established in the province of Quebec, Canada.

It was closed some years ago.

Hammer
A locality (population 65) in Roberts county, South Dakota, U.S.A.

In 1957 the name of the postmaster at Hammer was S. B. Hammer. This odd fact appears to have inspired the postmaster to produce a special and most unusual type of postmark (pictured below) in which three hammers are portrayed, one representing the name of the postmaster, and the others representing the name of his post office.

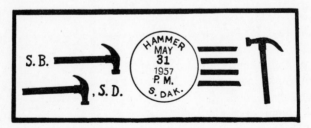

Happy Jack
Happy Jack is the name of a post office in Coconino county, Arizona, U.S.A.

Havelock
Marlborough district, South Island, New Zealand.

In August 1957 a newspaper agency report carried the story of how Mr. Bill Kenny, a Havelock mail bus driver, had undertaken the voluntary task of trying to discover the whereabouts of his town's post office which had somehow been 'misplaced' eighty years ago.

This was the story:

About the year 1877, Havelock, a rapidly-growing gold rush town, ordered a post office from England. But somewhere along the line the timber and plans for the new building were mixed up.

When Havelock put up its new post office several people pointed out that it looked like a church.

The explanation was simple. Havelock's post office looked like a church because it *was* a church.

The question, then, was: Where had the post office gone?

For eighty years one proud citizen after another has taken on the task of trying to find Havelock's lost post office. All have given up the hopeless search.

In 1957 Mr. Kenny renewed the quest. To find the lost post office he checked on every timber church throughout the country.

The latest report upon his activities was that in a remote and picturesque valley Mr. Kenny had found an ancient church with a strange appearance.

Was this Havelock's missing post office? And, if so, would the community owning it be prepared to exchange a church shaped like a post office for a post office shaped like a church?

Maddeningly, the report left unanswered these intriguing questions!

Hearts of Oak Benefit Society
The name of a sub-post office in the North-Western Head District of London, England.

105

Hell

A village (population 275) in Lanke canton Nord-Trondelag, central Norway, on Strinda Fjord, 16 miles east of Trondheim.

Hells Half Acre

A locality and summer post office in Natrona county, Wyoming, U.S.A. Near by is a petrified forest of sub-tropical trees estimated to be 50 million years old.

Highway Post Offices

A mobile postal service operated since 1941 in the United States of America in which motor vehicles are used for the collection and distribution of mail. The first service was operated between Washington, D.C., and Harrisburg, Virginia.

Special postmarks are used in which the abbreviation 'H.P.O.' appears together with the names of centres between which the service operates (e.g. Des Moines and Shenandoah, Iowa).

Holkham

Norfolk, England.

The post office at Holkham, Wells, Norfolk, is probably unique in that it is maintained at Holkham Hall, a private residence, the seat of the Earl of Leicester.

Here members of the public can purchase stamps and postal orders from a liveried servant of the Earl, serving behind a regulation post office counter.

The origin of this unusual post office goes back to the days of the eighteenth century when an ancestor of the Earl shared the office of Postmaster-General and established a post office on his Holkham estate for the convenience of his tenants and staff. In those days a mail coach called twice daily.

The postmark from this office bears the wording 'Holkham, Wells, Norfolk' and that of the neighbouring village post office 'Holkham Village, Wells, Norfolk.'

Hong Kong (Number of Post Offices)
British colony at the mouth of the Canton River, China.
Number of post offices (1952): ten.

Hope Bay
Hope Bay is a station established in the inhospitable Antarctic wasteland at Graham-land, a peninsula of the Antarctic continent.
The area is a Falkland Islands dependency.

Hospital postmarks
It would be possible to build an extensive collection of postmarks featuring naval, military, air force and civilian hospitals and sanatoria established in various parts of the world.
A brief list of some postal markings within this category is given below:

> Adelina Patti Hospital, Swansea, Wales.
> San Salvador Hospital, Rosales, San Salvador.
> Hospital Ship postmarks.
> Brisbane Base Hospital, Queensland, Australia.
> Christ's Hospital, Horsham, Sussex, England.
> State Sanatorium, Arkansas, U.S.A.
> U.S. Naval Hospital, Philadelphia, U.S.A.
> Shropshire Orthopaedic Hospital, Shrewsbury, England.
> Prince Albert Sanatorium, Saskatchewan, Canada.
> King Edward VII Sanatorium, Midhurst, Kent, England.
> Royal Hospital School, Ipswich, Suffolk, England.
> General Hospital, Calcutta, India.
> Hospital Sanatorio de Llanura, Argentina.

Hotel postmarks
Not many of the world's hotels can boast a 'personal postmark' of their own and even some of those which could formerly do so are now no longer in existence.

At one time several well-known hotels in India enjoyed the privilege of franking mail with their own postal imprint, among them the Savoy Hotel, Mussooree, the Maiden's Hotel, Delhi, the Grand Hotel, Calcutta, the Charleville Hotel, Mussooree, and the Burlington Hotel, Lucknow.

Similar facilities are – or in some cases *have* been – enjoyed by certain hotels in various other parts of the world, including the Banff Springs Hotel (Alberta, Canada), the Curtis Hotel (Minneapolis, U.S.A.), Shepheard's Hotel (Cairo, Egypt), the Raffles Hotel (Singapore, Malaya), Hotel Champlain, (New York, U.S.A.), Hotel Defreggerhof am Iselkerghe (Austria), the Formentol Hotel (Spanish Balearic Islands) and by three Italian hotels, the Albergo Dolomiti (Belluno), the Albergo Solda (Belluno), and the Albergo Molveno (Molveno-Trento).

A post office was opened at the Constant Spring Hotel, Jamaica, in December 1921, and date-stamps of the Langham Hotel, London, W., are known bearing the date 1931. A post office is also established at the Midland Hotel, Manchester.

House of Commons
London, S.W.1.

The Lower House of the British Parliament. A branch post office is open on weekdays during Parliamentary sessions.

Special postmarks are used at this branch office as they are for certain Dominion and Commonwealth Parliamentary establishments (e.g. House of Commons, Canada; Parliament House, Queensland, Australia, etc.).

House of Lords
London, S.W.1.

The Upper House of the British Parliament composed of Lords Spiritual and Lords Temporal.

A branch post office is established at the House of Lords, in the South-Western Head District of London, and outgoing correspendence is franked 'House of Lords, S.W.1.'

Houses of Parliament (South Africa)

A bi-lingual postmark, in English and Afrikaans, is in use at the Houses of Parliament post office, Cape Town, Union of South Africa.

Hungry Horse

A quaint cachet depicting a depressed and hungry-looking horse is sometimes imprinted on correspondence deriving from this town of 300 people, located near the newly-built Hungry Horse dam in Flathead county, Montana, U.S.A.

The legend is that in some bygone day a Red Indian party found a starving horse on the banks of the nearby creek. The Indians named the creek, one of the main inlets of the South Fork River, Hungry Horse Creek and when the township was founded in pioneer days it took its name from the adjacent creek.

Hutton Buscel

A parish and village in the North Riding of Yorkshire, 5 miles south-west of Scarborough. Population 300.

The name of Hutton Buscel is generally so spelt. In that form it appears on local signposts, on the Methodist chapel notice board and on a wayside seat 'Presented by the Hutton Buscel Pony Show, 1955'.

Only by the postal authorities – until March 1959 – was the name officially rendered in any other form. The post office apparently preferred 'Hutton Bushel' and so date-stamped correspondence for many years until pressure of opinion compelled a change.

By March 1959 the post office had come into line. On the sign outside the village post office the letter 'h' was painted out and replaced by a bright new 'c'.

And here is the story in postmark form:

I

Iceland (Number of Post Offices)
Independent island republic close to the Arctic Circle.
In 1952 there were 331 post offices in the republic.

Indonesia (Number of Post Offices)
Republic of S.E. Asia, formerly the overseas territory of The Netherlands.
Number of post offices (1952): 1,796.

'Industrial' postmarks
It is possible to build an interesting thematic collection of postmarks from sources having a strong connection with industrial and commercial activities.

There are, for example, many post offices in the north and northeastern districts of England which bear the names of well-known, or formerly well-known, collieries. Examples of these are Castle Eden Colliery, Easington Colliery, New Brancepeth Colliery, Blackhall Colliery and Bearpark Colliery (all in County Durham) and Shankhouse Colliery and Pegswood Colliery in Northumberland.

Other sources of industrial and commercial groups of postmarks are:

> Aycliffe Trading Estate, Co. Durham, England.
> Cowley Works, Oxford, England.
> Bata Estate, Essex, England.
> Kirkby Trading Estate, Liverpool, England.
> Fish Docks, Grimsby, England.
> British Industries Fair, Birmingham, England.
> Ardlethan Tin Mines, New South Wales, Australia.
> Andamooka Opal Fields, Australia.
> Perfect Pottery Works, Jubbulpore, India.
> Dehri Sugar Mill, Shahabad, India.

There are many other instances of postal place-names conforming to this theme including several communities in various parts of the world bearing the names Commerce and Industry.

110

'Initial' place-names

There are in the world a number of postal place-names derived from the initial letters of persons, cattle ranches, local industries, etc.

In the United States some towns have taken their names from the brand marks used on cattle. The town of Jay Em (J.M.) Wyoming, being an example of this. Pe Ell (Washington) was so named for a different reason. A French-Canadian by the name of Pierre settled here, but the Indians with whom he traded found his name impossible to pronounce. They called him Pe Ell ('P.L.') and later the town was named in his honour.

Other American instances of 'initial' place-names are: Arjay (Kentucky), Kaycee (Wyoming), and Kay Jay (Kentucky).

Canada has at least two similar examples of initial postal place-names. Ioco (British Columbia) represents the name of the Imperial Oil Company and Ceepeecee is so called from the initials of the Canada Packing Company, British Columbia, which operates a salmon cannery in the town.

There are also at least two initial postal place-names in Australia. They are Pee Dee, in New South Wales, and Dee Why in the same Australian state.

International Reply Coupons

International reply coupons are exchangeable in any member-country of the Universal Postal Union for a postage stamp, or postage stamps, representing the fee for a single-rate letter destined for a foreign country.

They are obtainable from most post offices in Great Britain at a cost (1960) of 1s. each and like Commonwealth Reply Coupons (q.v.) are a useful means of pre-paying the reply postage on letters from abroad.

International Stamp and Hobby Society (U.S.A.)

Caters for philatelists and postmark collectors. Provides facilities for the exchange of material and publishes a bulletin, 'The Stamp World'.

Secretary (1958): Nelson A. Frazar, P.O. Box 1, Desert Springs, California, U.S.A.

111

Island postmarks

Some collectors specialize in island postmarks from remote parts of the world. The scope for such a collection is wide and the field is a fascinating one, for postal facilities are available in some of the world's most inaccessible islands.

One difficulty in compiling a collection of island postmarks is that of defining the word 'island' in order to determine the limits of the collection.

A compromise solution to this problem is to limit the collection strictly to postmarks in which the word 'island' appears and a brief list of some postal place-names within this category is given below. The objection, however, to such a limitation is that it precludes the collection of postmarks from some of the well-known and most sought-after island postmarks (for example, Tristan da Cunha) in which the word 'island' is not incorporated.

Christmas Island	Nova Scotia, Canada
Christmas Island	Gilbert and Ellice Group
Christmas Island	Malaya
Norfolk Island	Australia
Pitcairn Island	Australia
Bow Island	Alberta, Canada
Sugar Island	Newry, Co. Down, Ireland
Minstrel Island	British Columbia, Canada
Holy Island	Berwick-on-Tweed
Canvey Island	Essex, England
Grand Island	Florida, U.S.A.
Pender Island	British Columbia, Canada
Bird Island	Minnesota, U.S.A.
Thursday Island	Queensland, Australia
Treasure Island	Florida, U.S.A.
Likoma Island	Nyasaland

Isle of Dogs

A London (England) sub-post office in the Thames-side metropolitan borough of Poplar.

Israel (Number of Post Offices)

Independent Asian republic.

Number of post offices (1952): 155.

Italy (Number of Post Offices)
Figures issued in 1937 gave the number of post offices in Italy as 11,344.
By 1952 the number had increased to 11,895.

J

Jamaica (Number of Post Offices)
British West Indies. Dependencies: Cayman Islands and Turks and
Caicos Islands.
Number of post offices (1952): 416.

Japan (Number of Post Offices)
Country of East Asia.
Number of post offices (1952): 15,314.

Jay Em
Jay Em, in Goshen county, Wyoming, U.S.A., owes its name to the
initials used as a cattle brand by an early pioneer.
In the 1880's a man named Jim Moore made a homestead on the
springs about two miles from the present site of Jay Em. His homestead
was called the J.M. Ranch and his cattle bore the J.M. brand.
About the year 1908 the community had grown and a request was
made for a post office to be opened. Mr. Lake C. Harris, who had
succeeded Moore as owner of the J.M. Ranch suggested the name
Jay Em for the new post office and the name was adopted.

Jean
A village in Clark county, Nevada, U.S.A., founded in 1906 by Mrs.
Jean Fayle, who opened a restaurant and post office on the Union
Pacific Railroad, and after whom the community was named.
In 1941 the village was moved from the railroad to U.S. Highway 91,
a distance of a quarter of a mile.
It lies 30 miles south of Las Vegas and consists of a garage, a
restaurant, a curio shop and a few homesteads. Rock (for roof tops)
is mined here and some of it is sent as far as Honolulu.

John o'Groats

A locality and post office on the north coast of Scotland, in Caithness; usually regarded as the northernmost point of the mainland of Great Britain.

It is said to have been named from an eight-sided house built by a Dutchman named Groat or Groot at the end of the fifteenth century.

Jugoslavia (Number of Post Offices)

Republic, south Europe.

Number of post offices (1952): 3,037.

Jump

Jump is the name of a locality and post office near Barnsley, Yorkshire, England.

A beck, or stream, which runs through the village of Jump forms the dividing line between the urban district councils of Hoyland and Wombwell. People used to jump over this beck and from this it is possible that the locality derived its name.

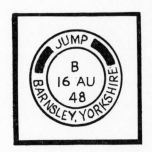

K

Kayenta

Navajo county, Arizona, U.S.A.

Claimed (1958) to be the most remote post office in the United States of America; 197 miles from the nearest railroad and telephone. Population: thirty-five.

Kew Gardens

The Royal Botanic Gardens at Kew, a few miles up the Thames from London, are visited every year by about 1,700,000 people.

The double-ring date-stamp of Kew Gardens, illustrated here, is obsolete as the office is now a sub-post office of Richmond, Surrey.

'Kicking mule' cancellation

A 'freak' postmark devised in the 1880's by an eccentric character named Klinkner.

Klinkner, a native of Oakland, California, manufactured metal signs, rubber stamps, and similar devices and was eventually persuaded to make cancellers for the postmasters of certain American towns, including Susanville, Forbestown, Goleta, and Port Townsend.

His postmark took the form of a mule with ears and tail and hind legs raised, and as the 'kicking mule' cancellation it attracted the attention of collectors as long ago as 1886 and has since been sought after by postmark enthusiasts in all parts of the world.

In more recent years Klinkner's curious cancellation became the subject of a book, *The Tale of the Kicking Mule*, by an American author, Lee H. Cornell.

Killer bar

A philatelic term denoting an adhesive postage stamp canceller, often of the 'barred' type, used as a means of defacing the stamps to prevent their re-use.

King and Queen Court House

A post office in King and Queen county, Virginia, U.S.A. In postmark form the name of the post office is abbreviated to 'King & Queen C.H.'

King of Prussia

A town and post office in Montgomery county, Pennsylvania, U.S.A.

L

Lake Winnipesaukee R.P.O.

A United States waterway mail service operated in New Hampshire under the control of the Railway Mail Service department.

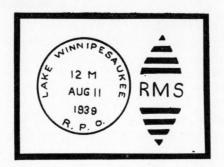

Landmark postmarks

Many of the world's most famous landmarks are featured in postmark form.

Among natural features throughout the world the following exist in postal date-stamp form:

Victoria Falls	Southern Rhodesia
Mount Gambier	South Australia
Table Mountain	Cape Province, South Africa
Niagara Falls	Ontario, Canada, and New York State, U.S.A.

Famous British landmarks available in postmark form include The Lizard, Giant's Causeway, Wookey Hole, John o'Groats, and Land's End.

There are also many postal date-stamps bearing the names of famous man-made landmarks, for example: Waltham Abbey (Essex, England), the Planetarium (New York, U.S.A.), Menai Bridge (Anglesey, Wales), the Golden Temple (Amritsar, India), Luqsor Winter Palace (Egypt), Parliament House (Sydney, Australia), Corfe Castle (Dorset, England) and the Empire State Building (New York, U.S.A.),

Land's End

A promontory on the Cornish coast traditionally regarded as forming the western-
most point of England.

The postmark of Land's End is unusual
because it joins the name of Sennen with
Land's End.

Laos (Number of Post Offices)

An independent sovereign state of S.E. Asia.

There were twenty-seven post offices in the country in 1952.

Last day postmark

A postmark bearing the date on which the office of origin ceased to
function. Alternatively, where a place-name change is involved, a last
day postmark might be one bearing the last date on which the old
place-name was in postal date-stamp use.

See: First day postmark.

Lebanon (Number of Post Offices)

Republic in the eastern Mediterranean.

Number of post offices (1952): 408.

Lilliput

In Swift's *Gulliver's Travels* the country of tiny inhabitants, Lilliput in
postmark form derives from a sub-post office in Poole, Dorset.

Another 'lilliputian' postmark was issued from 'the town of dwarfs',
Netherlands, in 1937.

Lizard, The

A peninsula to the south of Helford river in
south-west Cornwall, terminating 12 miles
south of Helston, in Lizard Point, the most
southerly promontory in England; altitude
186 feet.

Llanfairpwllgwyngyllgogerychwyrndrobwllllantysiliogogogoch
Although this fifty-eight-letter village on the A.5 road to Holyhead, Anglesey, possesses a post office its postmark appears in the abbreviated form, Llanfairpwll, Anglesey.

Loosely translated, the full name means 'St. Mary's Church in a hollow of white hazel, close to a rapid whirlpool and St. Tysilio's Church'.

The name is said to have been invented many years ago, as a tourist attraction, by a local tailor.

See 'Longest Place Names'.

Loggerheads
The dictionary defines the phrase 'to be at loggerheads' in this way:

'to quarrel; to be in contention about differences of opinion'.

In the geographical sense 'to be at Loggerheads' one need travel no further than a point in north-west Staffordshire, in Newcastle-under-Lyme rural district, where a locality 4 miles north-east of Market Drayton bears this name.

In postmark form, however, Loggerheads is at loggerheads with this tidy geographical arrangement. By its association with Market Drayton the postmark places Loggerheads, geographically in Staffordshire, in the neighbouring county of Shropshire!

London Apprentice
This curious postal place-name is borne by a locality near St. Austell, Cornwall, England.

London International Stamp Exhibition
Over two and a half million poundsworth of the world's most interesting and valuable postage stamps were among the 450 exhibits displayed

118

at the London International Stamp Exhibition which opened at Grosvenor House, Park Lane, London, W.1, on 6 May 1950.

Among many priceless exhibits were selections from the collection of King George VI and specimens from the G.P.O.'s own valuable storehouse of postal history treasures. The exhibition included displays by 185 United Kingdom and 167 overseas philatelists.

To mark the occasion a special double-ring date-stamp, as illustrated, was in use in which was incorporated an enlarged type of 'Maltese Cross' obliterator of similar pattern to those in use in Great Britain from 1840 to 1844.

Longest place-names

It is unfortunate, from the viewpoint of the collector, that some of the world's longest place-names are not perpetuated in postmark form.

The famous Welsh classic, Llanfairpwllgwyngyllgogerychwyrndrobwllllantysiliogogogoch, is an example of officialdom's deplorable lack of enterprise and imagination. As a date-stamp it appears in the abbreviated form 'Llanfairpwll, Anglesey' – an economy in metal at the expense of world renown.

Sutton-under-Whitestone-Cliffe, Thirsk, Yorkshire, is similarly afflicted. Letters posted in this charming village, at the foot of Sutton Bank with its one in four gradient, are date-stamped 'Sutton, Thirsk, Yorkshire', and with that the seeker of postal oddities must be content.

It would be interesting, but difficult, to discover which British postal date-stamp contains the most letters. The sub-post office date stamp of Willesden Avenue, Peterborough, Northants. (thirty-six letters) might be a claimant to the honour, but there may be other contenders with a stronger claim. Shankhouse Colliery, Cramlington, North'd. (thirty-five letters) comes close, and is followed by Over Stratton, South Petherton, Somerset (thirty-four letters).

119

But these claims to 'lettered' fame are dwarfed by some formidable contenders from overseas.

There is in New Zealand's North Island a village bearing the Maori name Taumatawhakatangihangakoauotamateaturipukakapikimaunga-horonukupokaiwhenuakitanatahu, claimed to be the longest place-name in the world. But, like its Welsh rival, this community is unable to offer postmark proof of its resounding claim to fame.

The township of Kleinfeltersville, a spot on the map in Lebanon county, Pennsylvania, is probably, with seventeen letters in its name, the longest *single* place-name to appear in postmark form in the United States of America but it is left to a rather dull-sounding American Navy postal station to provide what is probably, in America, the longest group of letters and numerals in postmark form. This postmark reportedly contains sixty-three letters and numerals comprising the words 'Field Branch, Bureau of Supplies and Accounts, Navy 10020 Sta., Cleveland, Ohio'. a lengthy effort equalled, but not eclipsed, by a bi-lingual souvenir date-stamp used at a philatelic exhibition held at Port Elizabeth, South Africa, in 1956, which carried the wording 'National Stamp Exhibition (Nasionale Posseeluitstalling) Port Elizabeth'.

Love

Replying to a correspondent's inquiry about his town the postmaster of Love (Butler county, Kentucky, U.S.A.) concluded:

'It's grand to be in Love!'

Loveland

In February 1959 the farming town of Loveland, in Larimer county, Colorado, U.S.A., became known as America's 'Sweetheart Town' – and it all began because romantic folk liked to have an appropriate postmark on the cards they sent out on St. Valentine's Day – 14 February.

For several years courting couples had been sending Valentine cards to Loveland, for postmarking and re-mailing.

In 1959 the idea became official and Valentine cards were put on the market with special double envelopes, the outer one addressed to Loveland post office.

Loveland's special postmark includes a drawing of Cupid, the Roman god of love.

Lovely Lane
The postmark of this romantic-sounding thoroughfare comes from Warrington, Lancashire, where an old-established sub-post office bears the name.

Lower Cape Bridgewater
Victoria, Australia.
> Claimed to be Australia's smallest post office.
> See: Smallest Post Office.

Lubec
Lubec (population 1,536), Washington county, Maine, is the location of the farthest east post office in the United States.

Luxembourg (Number of Post Offices)
Independent Grand Duchy adjoining Belgium.
> Number of post offices (1952): 121.

M

Macao (Number of Post Offices)
Overseas possession of Portugal in China, on the Canton River.
> Number of post offices (1952): three.

MacArthur
Raleigh county, West Virginia, U.S.A.
> The post office at MacArthur was officially opened on 15 April 1942

in response to a petition from residents in the region in honour of General Douglas MacArthur, then Supreme Commander of the Allied Forces in the southwest Pacific.

Madagascar (Number of Post Offices)
French overseas territory (with dependencies, including the Comoro Archipelago, Reunion, etc.).

Post offices in the territory (with dependencies) totalled 198 in 1952.

Maidens
An Ayrshire (Scotland) fishing village. Postal address: Maidens, Girvan, Ayrshire.

In April 1959 it was announced that the thirty-three-year-old Marquis of Ailsa had applied for the post of sub-postmaster at Maidens.

Lord Ailsa succeeded to the title in 1957 on the death of his father.

Maiden Voyage postmarks
Maiden voyage postmarks are something of a rarity and it is only with difficulty that their earliest use can be traced. It is possible that the earliest shipboard cancellation of this kind dates from 1905 when the White Star line were given permission for the use of a special postal cancellation.

The maiden voyage of the *Empress of Britain*, in April 1956, and of the *Empress of England*, in April 1957, had postal recognition and the voyage of *Mayflower II*, which sailed the Atlantic as a gift to the American people, was also postally commemorated.

Mailomat
An American coin-operated machine which permits the insertion of one or all of four different denominations of coin, the values of which are registered on a cash dial in front of the machine.

In this way the required postage value is dialled while the packets are fed successively into the posting aperture. By this system of mailing the letters are date-stamped and franked in one automatic operation as they are posted. Collection is effected by the postman from an aperture in the base of the machine.

122

Malaya (Number of Post Offices)
An independent monarchy within the British Commonwealth of Nations, consisting of eleven States: Johore, Kedah, Kelantan, Negri Sembilan, Pahang, Perak, Perlis, Selangor, Trengganu, Malacca, and Penang.

Number of post offices (1952): 355.

Malta (Number of Post Offices)
Mediterranean colony.

Number of post offices (1952): five.

Maltese Cross cancellation
The earliest postage stamps in the British Isles were cancelled with an obliterator inaccurately known as the Maltese Cross cancellation. Its general appearance more closely resembled that of a four-petalled Tudor Rose.

The so-called Maltese Cross obliterator was in general use from 1840 to 1844 in London, provincial districts of England and Wales and in Scotland and Ireland and isolated instances of its use occurred in certain centres in the 1870s.

A conventional type of Maltese Cross is also incorporated in contemporary postmarks from the George Cross island of Malta and it is interesting to compare the shape of this cross with that of the so-called Maltese Cross of the Victorian era.

Maritime Postmark Society (U.S.A.)
A non-profit international collectors' organization with members in more than twenty-five different countries.

Founded in 1939 and formerly known as the International Seapost

Cover Club, the society caters for beginners, average and advanced collectors and issues a bi-monthly journal, *The Seaposter*.

Marked Tree

The aborigine Indians in this section of Arkansas, U.S.A., marked a tree at the bend in the St. Francis River to indicate a crossing which saved 10 miles of up-river paddling.

In 1881 a camp was established on the site for the use of railroad workers. The camp was given the name Marked Tree and on its site today stands a prosperous little town of 1,000 people in a cotton-growing region.

Marshall, C. F. Dendy
(1872–1945).

Barrister-at-law, engineer and a specialist collector of material relating to British Postal History; M.A., Trinity College, Cambridge.

Mr. Dendy Marshall amassed a world-famous collection of material relating to the British post office. Author of *The British Post Office* (1926).

Martinique

An overseas department of France in the West Indies, area 386 sq. miles; pop. 240,000.

An ordinance of 4 March 1776 established a postal system in Martinique with offices at Saint Pierre, Fort de France (then known as Fort Royal), Trinité, and Marin. Probably the oldest known postmark from this island is the straight-line town mark of Saint Pierre. It dates from 1780.

Ma San
South Korea.

A centre of the South Korean textile industry. 'Ma' in Korean means 'horse' and 'San' means 'hill'.

Mauritius (Number of Post Offices)

An island colony in the Indian Ocean.

Dependencies include Rodrigues and a scattered group of coral islands in the Indian Ocean.

Number of post offices (1952): eighty-two.

Mecca

The post office at Mecca, Riverside county, California, U.S.A. (188 feet below sea level), is claimed to be the lowest permanent post office in the United States of America. Mecca is located about six miles north of Salton Sea, an inland lake 241 feet below sea level.

Metered mail

From 25 January 1912 a machine was in use at the General Post Office, London, whereby, when a letter and a coin had been inserted, a red franking mark bearing the words 'Postage Paid' was impressed on the letter. By this means the use of a postage stamp was obviated. The machine, which had been installed experimentally, was apparently not a success, for it was withdrawn from public use some months later.

The trial, nevertheless, has some significance to philatelists and postmark collectors, for it may well have foreshadowed some of the vast changes which future years may bring to the world's postal services. Already, to a considerable extent, the use of franking machines by Government departments and business houses has superseded the use of adhesive postage stamps and today millions of postal packets are pre-paid by the medium of the franking machine.

The first Government to authorize the substitution of franked impressions for postage stamps was that of New Zealand. In 1904 an early model of Mr. Ernest Moss's postal franking machine was placed on trial and proved to be satisfactory. Since that date great strides have been taken towards the perfection of high-speed machines capable of dispensing with the use of adhesive stamps. In 1920 Congress of the United States of America granted a licence to the Postage Meter Company for the use of an improved power-driven machine, and in May 1922 the use of the Pitney-Bowes machine was authorized by Great Britain's Postmaster-General.

From these beginnings the business use of automatic franking machines has developed to almost universal proportions, completely revolutionizing the despatch of mail in bulk.

Mexico (Number of Post Offices)

Federal republic of North America.

In 1952 there were 4,392 post offices in the country.

Midnight

The post office at Midnight, Humphreys county, Mississippi, U.S.A., was established about 1890.

The story concerning Midnight's name is that many years ago a number of plantation owners gathered for a poker game. These Southern gentlemen were somewhat wild and they often played for high stakes.

Finally, one unlucky player put up a large part of his land . . . and lost. The winner of the game pulled out his watch and said: 'Well, boys, it's midnight – and that's what I intend to call the piece of land I have won!'

This story has persisted throughout the years and when a post office was established on the land it was named Midnight.

Missionary packets

Many philatelic traders stock and sell 'missionary packets'. Their contents usually consist of adhesive postage stamps which have been torn or cut from correspondence, often complete with the accompanying postal markings. They are sold by packet price or weight and are often a useful means of obtaining postmarks from remote overseas regions.

Mis-spelling of place-names

See: Errors.

Mobile post offices

Covers and cards can sometimes be obtained with special postal markings which indicate that they have been handled by a mobile (motor vehicle) post office.

To France goes the credit for pioneering in October 1934 the mobile post office scheme. Britain's first mobile post office, of this type, was

introduced in September 1936; and in January, 1937, South Africa followed with the second mobile postal unit to be introduced in the British Empire.

Today many countries, including the United States of America, Switzerland, Denmark, Czechoslovakia, Australia, the Netherlands, and Germany, make use of 'post offices on wheels' for special occasions when on-the-spot postal facilities are required.

Money

A town and post office of Leflore county, Mississippi, U.S.A.

It was named in honour of the late Senator Hernando De Soto Money, a local landowner.

Montserrat (Number of Post Offices)

British island of the Leeward Group, West Indies.

Number of post offices (1952): fifteen.

Mooselookmeguntick

The name of a post office (no longer in existence) in Maine, U.S.A. The locality was named by an Indian hunter.

When asked, one day, how he had managed to shoot an outsize moose the Indian replied:

'Moose look. Me gun – tick!'

Morocco (Number of Post Offices)

Kingdom of North Africa.

Number of post offices, 1952 (excluding former Spanish Zone): 382.

In 1956 Spain conceded the independence of the former Spanish Zone in which, in 1952, there were forty post offices.

Mountain

To make a mountain out of a molehill is, traditionally, to make a lot of fuss about an unimportant matter.

In the geographical sense, however, the phrase may mean something quite different. A few years ago the inhabitants of Mole Hill (population

127

ninety-three), U.S.A., came to the conclusion that they did not like the name given to their home town.

They decided to change it.

Today letters deriving from this little community, in Ritchie county, West Virginia, bear the postmark of a new and more imposing name.

The new name?

Mountain.

Mount Gambier
A town at the foot of Mount Gambier, South Australia, in a rich pastoral and agricultural district near the border of New South Wales. Population: 7,000.

Mount Kosciusko Summit

In 1955 Australia's postmaster-general, Mr. Hubert Anthony, agreed to the establishment of a stone pillar box on the summit of Mount Kosciusko, Australia's highest peak, 7,308 feet above sea level, in the state of New South Wales.

When the box was cleared for the first time it was found to contain more than 2,200 items of mail, all of which received a special postmark. Now the box is cleared once a week during Australia's summer but in the winter drifting snow makes the collection of mail impossible.

The township of Mount Kosciusko at the foot of the mountain is 328 road miles from Sydney and has a population of about 300.

Mount Ruapehu Post Office

Officially named Mount Ruapehu Post Office, and situated on the northern slope of the mountain, 5,350 feet above Chateau Tongariro, is to be found New Zealand's highest post office, opened in 1958.

The post office is run by members of the Chateau mountain staff but it is a telephone office only and, despite its name, no postal business of any kind is handled.

Mozambique (Number of Post Offices)

Portuguese possession in East Africa.

Number of post offices (1952): 267

Much-travelled covers

Letters which go astray in the post are often productive of interesting postmark oddities.

One such letter, posted in Wakefield, Yorkshire, in September 1946, reached its destination, a local address, after journeying by way of New Zealand. The journey took four months and the packet eventually arrived decorated with an elaborate display of postmarks indicative of its strange wanderings.

Another much-travelled cover was the subject of a competition in a well-known British philatelic magazine. The envelope, addressed to a Mr. S. H. Ahmed at Kabuli Gate, Bombay, India, had passed from one 'Kabuli Gate' to another in search of the elusive Mr. Ahmed until, finally, almost black with superimposed postmarks, it had given up the abortive attempt to get itself delivered.

Ten years after the start of this extraordinary journey the envelope became the subject of a wartime competition in aid of the Red Cross and St. John's Ambulance Fund. Entrants were offered a prize for correctly estimating the number of postmarks, or part postmarks, shown in a photographic reproduction of the cover.

In 1947 a letter from the United Kingdom to Captain J. B. Cronin, H.Q., 64 Brigade Area, Maymyo, Burma, travelled throughout the length and breadth of India and Burma in search of its addressee. It finally reached Captain Cronin, now a West Midlands Gas Board official, in England, long after his demobilization from the army.

Even more widely travelled was a cover bearing a British King George V one penny postage stamp posted in Ealing, London, on 2 September 1913, addressed to 'Charles G. Hewitt, Apprentice,

S.S. *Queensland Transport*, Batavia, Java'. The cover turned up thirty-seven years later in a Leeds (Yorkshire, England) stamp dealer's shop containing fifteen postal endorsements including the postmarks of Batavia (27 September 1913), Singapore (13 October 1913), Kobe, Japan (4 November 1913), Osaka, Japan (8 November 1913), Ocean Island (20 December 1913) and several smaller places in the Netherlands East Indies.

One reason why letters go astray in this way is that people do not address them correctly. Here is an instance:

One day a clerk in a Northern Ireland bank began to address a letter to a client in Limavady, a small town less than twenty miles away.

Just as the clerk reached 'Lima . . .' the telephone rang and after answering it the clerk quite forgot to type the rest of the place-name on the envelope.

Six weeks later the letter was returned.

It had, of course, in the meantime been to Lima, Peru.

Mulberry
Mulberry (population 3,000) in Polk county, Florida, U.S.A., took its name from a mulberry tree which stood alone beside the railway line in a timber-producing area.

Around the tree grew the city of Mulberry. The tree is now battered scarred, and stunted but it still stands to remind the citizens of Mulberry of the days when the railroad men ordered goods to be dropped off 'at the Mulberry tree by the railroad'.

A Reproduction of the Mulready envelope.

POSTAGE ONE PENNY

Mulready envelope
An envelope with an elaborate pictorial design produced by the Irish-born painter, William Mulready, R.A. (1786-1863), for use in connection with the introduction of the penny postage system in 1840.

Mumps
A curiously-named locality in Oldham county borough, Lancashire, England.

Mystic
A pioneer map-maker wrote the word 'mystic' on a point of the map near this Black Hills region of South Dakota, U.S.A.

He intended to convey that a 'mistake' had been made but his spelling was somewhat erratic. Later map-makers took Mystic to be the name of the community – so Mystic was named by mistake!

Naval cancellations
From time to time naval cancellations have been used on the warships of many nations including those of Austria, France, Germany, Italy, and the United States of America.

As far as is known France and the U.S.A. are now the only nations using naval post offices with official postal cancellations.

The specimen illustrated is a French naval postmark from the warship *Richelieu*.

N

Netherlands (Number of Post Offices)
In 1952 there were 2,111 post offices in The Netherlands.
Postmarks were probably introduced about the year 1676.

Nevertire
A locality and post office in New South Wales
Australia.

New Caledonia (Number of Post Offices)
French overseas territory in the Pacific.
New Caledonia was discovered in 1774 and annexed by France
eighty years later. From 1871 to 1896 it was a convict settlement.
Dependencies of New Caledonia include the Isle of Pines, the
Wallis Archipelago, and the Huon Islands.
Post offices in the territory (with dependencies) totalled forty-three
in 1952.

New Invention
A sub-post office of Willenhall, Staffordshire, England, and locality
4 miles from Wolverhampton.

Nigeria (Number of Post Offices)
British colonial territory, West Africa.
Number of post offices (1952): 661.

'Noisy' postmarks
Among the 'queeriosity' groups an astute collector can gather are
postmarks from places bearing noisy names.

132

Here is a selection:

> Barking (Essex, England).
> Yelling (Huntingdon, England).
> Clatter (Montgomeryshire, Wales).
> Bangs (Texas, U.S.A.)
> Knock (Westmorland, England).
> Yap (Caroline Islands).
> Tooting (London, England).
> Boom (Belgium).

Nomansland

A locality and post office near Salisbury, Wiltshire, England.

Nome

A former gold-rush town on the north shore of Norton Sound, Alaska.

Nome, formerly Anvil City, was established in 1899, and is said to have been named by mistake.

It appears that the British survey ship *Herald* was making a chart of this part of the Alaskan coast, various names being inserted on the chart, where known.

At what is now known as Cape Nome the map-maker wrote 'Name?' intending to have the correct name inserted later. When the rough map was copied a draughtsman transcribed the scrawled query as Nome – and that is the name which appears on postmarks from this Alaskan city today.

North Borneo (Number of Post Offices)

Colony on the northern part of the island of Borneo. Became a Crown Colony, with the island of Labuan, on 15 July 1946.

In 1951 there were eleven post offices in the territory.

Northern Rhodesia (Number of Post Offices)
A region north of the Zambesi, South Africa. From 1953 became a unit of the Federation of Rhodesia and Nyasaland.
Number of post offices (1952): seventy-nine.

North Pole (U.S.A.)
A rural station post office of Colorado Springs, El Paso county, Colorado, U.S.A.
A special metered cancellation is in use at this office incorporating a pictorial design and the slogan 'Home of Santa's Workshop'.

Norway (Number of Post Offices)
Constitutional monarchy of N. Europe on the Scandinavian peninsula.
Number of post offices (1952): 4,874.

Numeral postmarks
Numbered obliterators were in use in various forms in Great Britain approximately from 1844 to 1906. (See Duplex mark.)
Another form of numeral postmark is represented by places bearing 'numeral names'. There are several such places in various parts of the world. Here is a list of some of them:

Number One, Consett, Co. Durham, England.
Figure Five, Arkansas, U.S.A.
Six, West Virginia, U.S.A.
One-Four, Alberta, Canada.
Twentysix, Kentucky, U.S.A.
Forty Four, Arkansas, U.S.A.
Fifty Six, Arkansas, U.S.A.
Eighty Four, Pennsylvania, U.S.A.
Eighty Eight, Kentucky, U.S.A.
Ninety Six, South Carolina, U.S.A.

Nyasaland (Number of Post Offices)
British Protectorate, Central Africa.
In 1893–94 twenty-four post offices were opened in the territory. The number of post offices in 1952 was fifty-five.

134

From 1953 became part of the Federation of Rhodesia and Nyasaland.

Nykobing Jubilee Fête
A special postmark was issued, in August 1939, from a mobile post office unit in attendance at the Nykobing Jubilee Fête, Denmark. Letters and cards were franked with an oval postmark.

Odd and Odder
Odd is the name of a post office in Raleigh county, West Virginia, U.S.A.

Odder is the name of a post office in Aarhus province, Denmark.

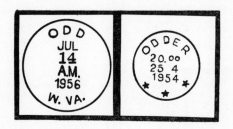

Old Harry
Old Harry (Province of Quebec, Canada) owes its curious name to an early settler whose Christian name was Harry.

Olympic Games postmarks
Special postmarks of many varied types have been used from time to time in connection with the modern revivals of the Olympic Games.

135

The examples illustrated show types of postmarks used at Wembley, Great Britain, in 1948, and at Helsingfors, Finland, in 1952.

For the XVI Olympiad held at Melbourne, Australia, in 1956, a special village was built to house contestants complete with its own post office and Olympic Village postmark.

One Day postmark

At the opening of the Beit Bridge across the Zambesi on 24 May 1939, the post office authorities of Southern Rhodesia opened a special post office for the day on which the opening ceremonies took place.

The postmark, a double ring type with the place-name 'Chirundu' above and 'Southern Rhodesia' below, was virtually a 'first day' and a 'last day' specimen and, as such, is an item of considerable rarity and value.

One Hundred Mile House

A small town in British Columbia, Canada, 100 miles from Lillooet, from which fact the name is derived. Population (1957) about 200 but because of the rapid expansion of the local lumber industry the town is often referred to as 'the fastest-growing community in British Columbia'.

P

Painted Post

A village in Steuben county, New York, U.S.A.

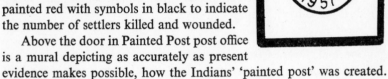

The village derives its name from the fact that after a battle between Mohawk Indians and whites the Mohawk war chief caused a tree to be felled, hewed four square, and painted red with symbols in black to indicate the number of settlers killed and wounded.

Above the door in Painted Post post office is a mural depicting as accurately as present evidence makes possible, how the Indians' 'painted post' was created.

Pakistan (Number of Post Offices)

From 23 March 1956 an Islamic republic within the British Commonwealth.

Number of post offices (1952): 7,552.

Paquebot

A cancellation applied, in general, at the port of arrival to letters posted on board ship.

Paradise

Paradise is a popular postal place-name: at least fourteen towns and villages bearing this name are to be found in different parts of the world.

Paradise, Montana, U.S.A., was so named because it has a comparatively milder winter than the rest of Montana.

Paradise, Pennsylvania, U.S.A., was formerly known as Dog Town because there were so many dogs there. When the canine population was reduced the residents of Dog Town are said to have given a sigh of relief – and renamed their town Paradise.

In Welsh the name is rendered Paradwys and there is one post office so named in Anglesey.

England's only postal Paradise is situated in Warwickshire. It is a sub-post office in Coventry.

Pearson Hill 'Opera Glass cancellation

A distinctive type of postmark produced by an early type of cancelling machine invented by Mr. Pearson Hill, son of Sir Rowland Hill, in 1857.

The machine produced a curious 'Siamese twin' type of postmark consisting of two joined circles, giving some resemblance to an 'opera glass'.

Peculiar

A community in Cass county, Missouri, U.S.A., about twenty-five miles south of Kansas City.

Penny Postage Jubilee

A special postmark was in use in 1890 in connection with the Penny Postage Jubilee. It bore the wording 'Penny Postage Jubilee 1840–1890, South Kensington'.

Personal postmarks

An amusing variation of the postmark theme is to attempt to obtain

138

date-stamps from places bearing one's personal Christian name and surname and the names of one's friends or relatives.

There are in the world thousands of post offices bearing 'personal postmark' names of this type. Norman Wells (Northwest Territories, Canada), Hazel Grove (Stockport, Cheshire, England), Christina Lake (British Columbia, Canada), and Roy Hill (Western Australia) are examples of the case where a *single* postal place-name incorporates a Christian name and a surname.

To achieve the 'date-stamp doubles' of more difficult name-combinations it may be necessary to obtain two separate postmarks:

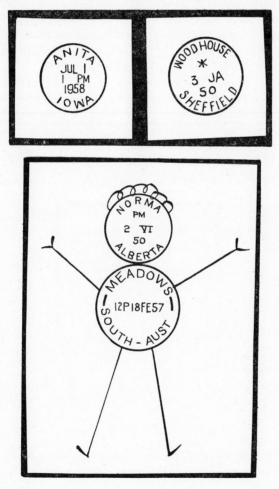

one for the first, or Christian name; another for the second name or surname.

It is possible to contrive 'Peeky Postmarks', a lighthearted sideline in this collecting pastime, by joining two 'name' postmarks to form a head and body, afterwards etching in arms and legs and hair to form an amusing version of the 'personal postmarks' idea. Examples of both these ideas are illustrated on page 139.

Philatelic Congress and Exhibition postmarks
In recent times special postmarks have been in use the world over to commemorate large philatelic gatherings and special philatelic occasions.

With the exception of certain wartime years a Philatelic Congress has been held annually in Britain since the First Postage Stamp Exhibition and Congress held in Manchester in 1909.

On these occasions postmarks of special design are often used. For the London International Stamp Exhibition, held at Grosvenor House, Park Lane, London, from 6 May to 13 May 1950, for example, a large double-ring date-stamp and a Maltese Cross type of canceller were in use.

Philatelic occasions in other countries have been similarly productive of interesting date-stamps of varied types.

Philometer Society, The
An American society devoted to the interests of collectors of machine meter marks. Publishes a monthly bulletin, *The Philometerist*.

Picture Postcards
Picture postcards were first devised by a French stationer, Besnardeau, for the use of soldiers during the Franco-Prussian war. They featured

war-like themes and sold in thousands, but after the defeat of the French forces interest in them lapsed.

Later, a more picturesque type of viewcard was introduced by Bertanza but in Britain privately-issued picture cards – views of Edinburgh – did not make their appearance until 1894.

Today the yearly average output from leading British firms is in the region of 100 million cards.

In bygone days there was a tremendous vogue for the hobby of postcard collecting. One man had views of almost every beauty spot in the civilized world and his collection totalled 163,000 items. It is from hoards of this type, and from collections on a much smaller scale, that much valuable postmark material may be derived. Postcards gathered in this way, and now discarded, invariably carry interesting postal markings many of them from sources no longer in existence.

Picture postmarks

In 1949 the American magazine *Collier's Weekly* offered 25-dollar awards for each published 'picture postmark' consisting of two or more postmarks so arranged as to create an idea.

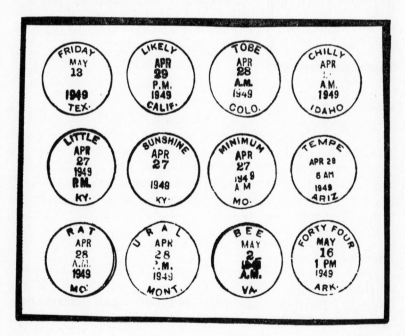

Actual postmarks had to be submitted and there were many amusing entries.

Using five different postmarks from towns in five widely-separated states one entrant contrived the sentence 'Only Alert Crooks Locate Money'. Another ingenious contributor, using four postal date-stamps, devised the humorous observation 'Hi Hat Smiths Turn Out To Be Ordinary' and yet another competitor contrived the cautionary comment 'Check Speed Busy Thorofare Lookout Kidds Crossing Street' – all from postmarks.

There were many other picture postmark entries. One, from an Arkansas entrant, ran 'Ima Busy Little Bee Ina Clover Field'; another said 'Lovely Maiden Hooks Rich Batchelor', the words representing postmarks from, respectively, Kentucky, North Carolina, Texas, Mississippi, and Louisiana.

Piggs Peak
A small town (white population 100) in a forest area of Swaziland, South Africa.

Pillar box
Pillar boxes (or mailing boxes) were first used in France. They owe their introduction in Britain to Anthony Trollope, an inspector of postal deliveries who was later to become famous as a novelist.

The first British pillar boxes were brought into use at St. Helier, Channel Islands, on 23 November 1852, almost a year after Trollope had first advocated their use. Similar boxes were introduced in Guernsey in the following year and, thereafter, were adopted generally in Britain.

Pitcairn Island
A British island in the eastern Pacific, discovered by Captain Carteret, of H.M.S. *Swallow*, on 2 July 1767, and named after one of his lieutenants. It remained unoccupied until 1790 when it was taken over by mutineers of H.M.S. *Bounty* accompanied by natives from Otaheite.

142

In 1856 the inhabitants, numbering 192, were evacuated at their own request to Norfolk Island but later forty of them returned to Pitcairn. The islands of Henderson, Ducie, and Oeno were annexed to Pitcairn in 1902.

Until 1927 there was no official post office on the island and letters, bearing a rubber-stamp inscription 'Posted at Pitcairn Island: No Stamps Available', were handed to the captains of passing ships. In June 1927 a New Zealand postal agency was established on the island and thirteen years later the first post office was opened.

Plot Night postmarks
Among postal place-names with a Gunpowder Plot connection are several bearing the name Guy and one, in Kentucky, named Squib.

Fireworks (Illinois, U.S.A.) is a branch office of East Saint Louis; Bangs is the name of a community in Brown county, Texas.

Pole Station, Antarctica
In 1957–58 a post office was established at the South Pole by the United States Navy as part of 'Operation Deepfreeze' in connection with the International Geophysical Year.

The tiny post office – a corner of the mess less than 10 ft. square – became a target of postage stamp and postmark collectors the world over. People stirred by curiosity wrote to the station to inquire how its eighteen inhabitants were finding life in the world's most hostile climate. The philatelic part of the operation became so heavy that the Navy had to impose a limit of five letters for each collector.

Pony Express
An early overland mail system inaugurated in U.S.A. on 3 April 1860.

It ran from St. Joseph, Missouri, to the Pacific coast, a distance of 1,950 miles covered by relays of riders famed for their hardihood and courage. The time schedule demanded coverage of 200 miles every twenty-four hours, day and night, summer and winter. There were about 80 riders, 500 horses and 190 relay stations covering the service and during the sixteen months it was maintained only one mail pouch was lost.

'Buffalo Bill' (William Frederick Cody), the American scout and, later, organizer of the famous Wild West Show, served the Pony Express as a rider while still in his teens.

Covers borne by the Pony Express carried special postal markings and are now highly prized philatelic treasures.

Portugal (Number of Post Offices)
Independent republic of S.W. Europe.

Number of post offices (1952): 9,057.

Portuguese Guinea (Number of Post Offices)
An overseas province of Portugal on the west coast of Africa.

Number of post offices (1952): twenty-three.

Portuguese India (Number of Post Offices)
Portuguese possessions consisting of the State of Gôa, and the islands of Angediva, São Jorge, and Morcegos on the coast of the Arabian Sea; Damão, Dedra, and Nagar-Aveli on the Gujerat coast; the islands of Diu, Gogola and Simbor.

Number of post offices in the territory (1952): eighty-seven.

Postal Cancellation Society (U.S.A.)
A postmark collectors' society founded in the U.S.A. in 1935. Merged with the Postmark Collectors' Club (q.v.) in February, 1950.

144

Postal History Society, The
This society was inaugurated in 1936 with the object of co-ordinating the researches of postal history students.

The society publishes a quarterly bulletin and monthly meetings are held in London.

Postal slogans
In December 1917, when such newspaper headlines as 'RUSSO-GERMAN ARMISTICE SIGNED' and 'LIQUID FIRE ATTACK AT CAMBRAI' were typifying the grim trials of war, a certain British postal innovation passed practically unnoticed. In that month were introduced the first of a series of three machine-franked slogans urging the public to 'Buy National War Bonds'.

The precedent for this enterprising move lay deeply rooted in the fertile soil of post office initiative. More than 250 years earlier, letters passing through the Kent post had borne this quaintly-worded inscription:

> The Post
> For All Kent
> Goes Every
> Night From
> The Round Ho-
> -use in Love
> Lane & Comes
> Every Mor-
> ninge

In the interval since 1661, however, when this impression was extant, no apparent use was made of the publicity potentialities of the postal imprint.

Revived in the stress of war, the slogan had nevertheless come to stay. Although its wartime use lapsed with the cessation of hostilities in 1918, a new patriotic use was found for it eight years later when employers of labour were postally encouraged to 'Join the King's Roll and Employ War Disabled Men'.

From these beginnings emerged a long stream of postal slogans, the collection and study of which has provided unbounded opportunities for collectors in all parts of the world.

In February 1922 British postal slogans were inviting people to 'Visit The British Industries Fair' – an enjoinder which, with varied wording, has encouraged attendance at this exhibition on many succeeding occasions. The years 1926 and 1927 witnessed the zenith of a drive to popularize British goods, and in this cause the postal legends were again vociferous. 'British Goods Are Best', ran one official proclamation. Another, used in the G.P.O. Foreign Section, enjoined overseas buyers to 'Buy British Made Goods'.

Then followed a determined Post Office campaign to induce the public to become telephone-minded. For several years internal mail bore such messages as 'Shop By Telephone', 'Get The Telephone Habit', 'Trade Follows The Phone', and, with inspired pungency, 'You Are Wanted On The Phone'.

To these could be added innumerable examples from more recent times. 'Save For The Silver Lining' came out in support of the National Savings Campaign, and 'Take No Chances – Keep Death Off The Road' in connection with a British road safety campaign. On other occasions members of the public have been postally encouraged to 'Volunteer For A Forces Career', 'Take Staggered Holidays For Comfort', 'Lend A Hand On The Land', 'Save Waste Paper For Salvage', 'Keep Food Premises Clean'. 'Grow More Food'. 'Eat Apples For Health', 'Fly By British Air Lines', 'Post Early For Christmas', and, with the hurried impartiality of machines franking between 300 and 900 letters a minute, to 'Dig For Victory' and 'Pray For Peace'. In April 1959 Britain's G.P.O. hopefully introduced verse into its slogans by franking correspondence with these wishful sentiments:

> Correct Addressing
> What a Blessing
> Saves Us Guessing

Overseas countries have adopted the slogan idea with perhaps even greater versatility.

Apart from such conventional examples as 'Visit Ostend The Queen of Seaside Resorts' – a bi-lingual invitation franked on Belgian correspondence – there are to be found a large number of artistic pictorial slogans from Switzerland tempting one, for example, to '*Séjournez à Genève*', while other Swiss, Dutch, Danish, and French centres have issued attractive designs bearing heraldic devices, humorous cartoons and slogan-supported imprints of a similar character.

New Zealand post offices, using a distinctive type of continuous-impression cancellation, are given excellent opportunities for domestic and overseas propaganda. 'Your Telephone Will Reach Your Friend In The Other Island' claims one imprint from this source. Even Gibraltar, stolid bastion of Mediterranean respectability, has had recourse to the advantages of postal advertising. A slogan neatly incorporated into the date-stamp claims for The Rock that it is 'The Travel Key of the Mediterranean', and this example, used in 1932, has no doubt been succeeded by others.

Elsewhere the slogan (the word derives from the Gaelic *sluaghghairm* and originally referred to the war-cry of the old Highland clans) has been adapted to meet local and specific needs. By means of it Mexico has proclaimed the evils of alcoholism and Trinidad the virtues of her sugar. As early as 1912 Canadian post offices were using slogans. An example of that year was a slogan reading 'Vancouver Mid-Summer Fair Aug. 10–17, 1912'. Since that date Canadian postal slogans have urged the public to 'Give To Conquer Cancer', 'Eat Right For Health', 'Observe Sunday', 'Be Friendly And Courteous To Tourists', 'Come To The Boys' And Girls' Fair', 'Help Prevent Forest Fires', 'Support The Blood Donor Campaign', and to 'Pay No More Than Ceiling Prices'. A Canadian slogan used in 1956 asserted, 'For The Greatest Year Of Your Life – Join The Army'; another, used in 1958, declared somewhat enigmatically: 'Why Wait For Spring? Do It NOW!' For overseas consumption the Dominion has made use of such postal invitations as 'Holiday This Year In Canada', and 'Canada's Doors Are Open To Tourists'.

Fijian meter marks have suggested 'Follow The Sun To Fiji' and the former Free City of Danzig issued a slogan which declared 'Without A Newspaper You Live In The Moon'. On the other side of the world British Guiana has been postally persuasive on the subject of Demerara coffee, while Palestine (now the state of Israel) at one time tri-lingually metered her mail with messages regarding the merits of Jaffa oranges.

Bush fires and War Bonds, traffic dangers and trade fairs, black market activities and noisy radio sets have all, at one time or another, been appropriately commended or condemned by this versatile postal medium – a medium which has itself not always remained immune from criticism as when, from behind the crumbling façade of Hitler's Third Reich, it was used by the Nazi postal authorities to propagate war-hate and, in 1949, by Britain to say 'Thank You For Food Gifts'. On one occasion, in Canada, indiscreet use of the slogan 'It's Quicker To Telegraph' caused amusement and some resentment when it was impressed on letters carried on a pioneer air mail flight.

147

Whatever the merits of its use and the demerits of its abuse, this steady stream of postal persuasion and propaganda holds attractive possibilities for the specialist collector.

The scope is wide, the interest unending, and it may well be the case that material now easily acquired may possess considerable rarity value in the course of time.

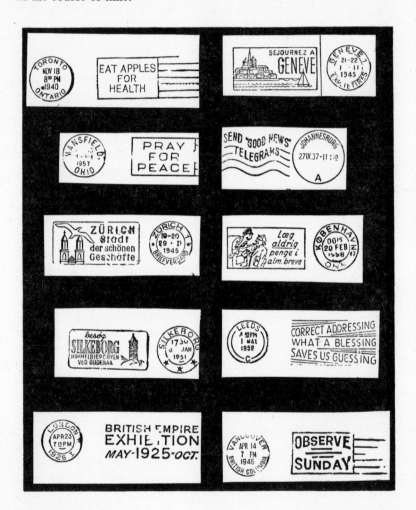

Postmark Club, The

The Postmark Club, founded in 1883 with an original membership of about twenty, is a private association for promoting the study and collection of postmarks.

Packets containing members' contributions for exchange are circulated by post.

Hon. secretary (1960): R. Ward, 48 Banner Cross Road, Ecclesall, Sheffield, 11.

Postmark Collectors' Club (U.S.A.)

An international organization of collectors of postmarks, all types of postal cancellations, postal markings and allied items.

Founded by the late Charles E. Strobel, of Cleveland, Ohio, in 1943. The society issues a monthly bulletin, first published in October 1947. Club director: Rev. Walter A. Smith, P.O. Box 355, Bath, Maine, U.S.A.

Postmark party games

Several amusing party games can be devised by means of postmarks.

Here are four examples:

(1) Prepare for each contestant an envelope containing twelve assorted postmarks from any part of the world. When all are ready, contestants open their envelopes and are asked to sort the postmarks in north to south order, according to the map location of the place-names. Only the postmarks of prominent places should be used and the correct north to south order should be determined beforehand by means of an atlas.

(2) An 'introductory' party game. Mount on cardboard the postmarks of several places of somewhat similar names (e.g. Blackpool, Pontypool; Harwich, Norwich). Cut the mounted postmarks carefully in half, giving to each guest one half of a postmark. Guests must discover who holds the corresponding half of their postal place-name.

(3) A biographical postmark game. Cut out and mount on separate postcards the postal date-stamps of places strongly connected with prominent persons (for example, the postmarks of Dublin and Ayot St. Lawrence might be chosen to represent George Bernard Shaw). With these postal place-names to guide them, contestants must determine the name of the famous person represented by the postmarks on each card.

(4) Obtain from newspapers and magazines easily-identified pictures of prominent places (e.g. Eiffel Tower, Blackpool Tower, New York's Empire State Building). Mount these pictures and give them an identifying letter (A, B, C, etc.).
Obtain, and mount on cardboard, postmarks to correspond with the

pictures (Paris, Blackpool, New York, etc.) and number these 1, 2, 3 and so on.

Contestants are then required to 'match up' correctly each picture with its appropriate postmark.

'Postmark U.K.'

A radio programme prepared by the B.B.C.'s North American Service for Canadian listeners; introduced in May 1951.

Postmark values

It is only in relatively recent times that any serious attempt has been made to set a market price upon the value of postal markings.

For many years Britain's Postmark Club, encouraging interest in the exchange and valuation of items, used as a basis among its members a unit called a 'mark'. A 'mark' was equal to one-sixth of a penny, and it was at one time quite possible to buy interesting and sometimes quite rare material at prices varying from one 'mark' to, say, twenty-four 'marks' – the latter price, of course, being equal to fourpence.

By the middle 1930's, however, interest in postal markings, and notably in pre-stamp letters, had reached a stage where public auctions of material other than adhesive postage stamps were deemed to be merited. Reporting one such auction the London *Sunday Times* of 11 October 1936 stated:

'Thirty philatelists, three of them women, spent yesterday afternoon in a London saleroom bidding at the first auction ever held of rare postal marks. Postmarks date back to the middle of the seventeenth century and were the receipt stamps for postages due before the coming of the adhesive stamp. Because nobody knows their value, these early bidders at the first auction sale were able to secure marks for a few shillings which may later realize hundreds of pounds. . . .'

In spite of the relatively low prices obtaining at the time, however, the middle 1930's saw the beginning of a definite commercial interest in postmark valuation.

In 1936, at a saleroom near Oxford Circus, the collection of one of Britain's foremost postmark enthusiasts, the late Mr. J. H. Daniels, of Brighton, came up for sale. For many years Mr. Daniels had pioneered in this field of philatelic study. He had become well known as an authority on his subject and as a guide and kindly counsellor to collectors of British postmarks. His collection, representing a lifelong

150

labour on a subject close to his heart, contained hundreds of thousands of items, including a fine series of 'Bishop Marks' from 1663 onwards and a contemporary official proclamation announcing the appointment of Henry Bishop, of Henfield, Sussex, to the post, on 16 January 1660, of His Majesty's Postmaster-General.

The total collection, at a time when public interest in postal markings was just beginning to make itself apparent, realized a little over £1,100.

But this was merely a beginning.

In 1945 a London firm offered for sale the notable collection amassed by the late Mr. C. F. Dendy Marshall. The collection virtually amounted to a complete history of the British Post Office. It included practically everything connected with the carriage of mails that could conveniently be housed in an individual collection.

The sale realized nearly £10,000. For one item, a 'wreck' cover of 1875, sent from London to the United States, a price of £17 was reached. For a single postmarked envelope of 1876, despatched from the United States Consulate at Callao, Peru, to an address in Georgia, the sum of £30 was paid. A collection of English and 'used abroad' cancellations and adhesives found a purchaser at £235.

Since that date the value of money has fallen and prices have risen correspondingly. Thus, a single envelope of 1872 from the collection of the late Mr. E. Egley, of Leeds, realized £775 at an auction in London in 1952 because of its rare and exotic postal markings.

From such figures it is possible to trace the rapid growth of interest in a hobby which at one time could claim to be no more than philately's Cinderella sister.

Post Office Magazine

Published monthly by H.M. Postmaster-General at the Post Office Headquarters, London, E.C.1, price 3d.; yearly subscription (1960) 4s.

This official publication contains many interesting background facts, articles, photographs, etc., concerning British post offices, postal history and other postal matters.

Pre-cancels

Pre-cancels are postage stamps bearing machine-printed cancellation marks, issued in complete sheets to business firms, etc., to facilitate speedy handling of the mail at post offices.

Modern pre-cancels bear the name of the place of posting and they are used extensively in many countries including the United States, Canada, Austria, France, the Netherlands, and Belgium.

They make an interesting study and are collected by many specialists in the field.

Pressmen's Home

Pressmen's Home, Tennessee, U.S.A., is the headquarters of the International Printing Pressmen and Assistants' Union of North  America, a self-contained community established in 1910 and now occupying an estate of 3,160 acres in the mountains of East Tennessee.

Although it is not an incorporated city, Pressmen's Home has a tuberculosis sanatorium, an hotel, a memorial chapel, a 650,000-gallon swimming pool, a dairy barn and pasteurization plant, forty residences, a technical school and a post office, whose postmark is illustrated.

The community is organized for the service, protection and technical education of all pressroom workers in North America and courses of practical instruction in all phases of press work are conducted in the technical school for the benefit of the union's members.

Puskin Anniversary postmark

In 1949 a special postmark was issued in Prague, Czechoslovakia, to commemorate the 150th anniversary of the birth, in Moscow on 26 May 1799, of Alexander Sergeyevich Puskin (or Pushkin) the celebrated Russian poet.

R

Rainier III

Prince of Monaco since 1949.

A special pictorial postmark was in use on 19 April 1956, to commemorate Prince Rainier's marriage with Grace Patricia Kelly (Princess Grace of Monaco).

Randsburg

A small mining town deep in the heart of California, U.S.A.

The first post office was opened here on 16 April 1896.

Some years ago, when the postmaster announced his intention of retiring, the authorities appointed a successor before the other man was ready to relinquish his duties. So indignant was the original postmaster at what he deemed to be unfair treatment that he refused to cease business and for a time there was a possibility that two post offices, virtually next door to each other, would continue to offer service to the public.

Apparently, however, the crisis was averted because both post offices were never in use at the same time.

Red Devil

A small mining town (pop. approximately 100) on the Kuskokwim River, midway between McGrath and Bethel, Alaska, U.S.A.

There has been an active mining camp at Red Devil since 1942 and the post office was established there on 28 October 1957.

Reversible place-names

Postmarks offer interesting evidence of the existence of many places in the world whose names are the same when read backwards or forwards.

Ada (Kansas, U.S.A.) and Aba (Nigeria) are simple examples of this, but there are instances of longer place-names of the same, or similar, type. Tumut (New South Wales, Australia) is one such name; Lal Lal (Victoria, Australia) and Aramara (Queensland, Australia) are further examples from the same continent. Along the same lines are Navan (Ontario, Canada) and Glenelg (Kyle, Ross-shire, Scotland).

There are also instances of 'twin towns' whose names are merely reversed versions of the same name. Thus, Alton is a town in Alabama, U.S.A., and Notla is a community in Texas, U.S.A. Walker (Arkansas) and Reklaw (Texas) have a similar kinship and Colver and Revloc, two small mining towns in Pennsylvania, U.S.A., share the same reversible place-name affinity.

Rhydwyn
Anglesey, Wales.

This Welsh village formerly appeared as Rhydwen ('white ford') in postmark form, but the ford (or stream) was originally named after a certain Mr. Wyn. When this explanation was given to the postal authorities they readily agreed to revert to the old, correct spelling – Rhydwyn.

Rocket posts
The conveyance of mail by means of rockets is a relatively new innovation. Early experiments were carried out in Germany by Herr G. Zucker who was later granted facilities for extensive experiments at Rottingdean (Sussex), the Hebrides and at Lymington (Hampshire) in 1934.

A special cancellation was used in connection with these tests and on one occasion when correspondence was damaged at the Hebrides trials owing to a premature explosion the covers were endorsed 'Damaged by explosion at Scarp-Harris'.

154

Rogue River mailboat service
A daily service operated by specially designed boats with 52 h.p. outboard motors up the treacherous Rogue River in Oregon, U.S.A., on a 32-mile route from Gold Beach to Agness.

The route covers some of the roughest terrain in the United States where roads are non-existent and resort has had to be made to the roaring current and thundering rapids of the river as a means of communication.

In addition to serving Agness, a small resort community of a dozen or so families in Curry county, the motorboat mail service caters for a number of summer retreats and prospectors who live in country that can only be seen by hiking through the trails, or from an aeroplane or from the river boat.

Rough and Ready
Rough and Ready, Nevada county, California, U.S.A., owes its curious name to General Zachary ('Rough and Ready') Taylor (1784–1850), who became the twelfth President of the United States in 1848.

In former days the town of Rough and Ready was a famous gold-mining centre with a population of approximately 5,000. In 1956 its population was 130.

Royal Air Force stations
There are several Royal Air Force station post offices in the United Kingdom the postmarks of which make an interesting addition to a collection of date-stamps connected with the fighting services.

Here is a list of some of the stations at which post offices have been established:

Abingdon R.A.F. Station, Abingdon, Berkshire.
Bassingbourn R.A.F. Station, Royston, Hertfordshire.
Bridgnorth R.A.F. Station, Bridgnorth, Shropshire.
Finningley R.A.F. Station, Doncaster, Yorkshire.
Faldingworth R.A.F. P.O., Lincoln.

Gaydon R.A.F. Station, Leamington Spa, Warwickshire.
Hemswell R.A.F. Station, Gainsborough, Lincolnshire.
Honington Camp, Bury St. Edmunds, Suffolk.
Lindholme R.A.F. Station, Doncaster, Yorkshire.
Little Rissington R.A.F. Station, Cheltenham, Glos.
Marham R.A.F. Station, King's Lynn, Norfolk.
Newton R.A.F. Station, Nottingham.
St. Eval R.A.F. Station, Wadebridge, Cornwall.
St. Mawgan R.A.F. Station, Newquay, Cornwall.
Sculthorpe R.A.F. Station, Fakenham, Norfolk.
Upavon R.A.F. Station, Pewsey, Wiltshire.
Upwood R.A.F. Station, Huntingdon.
Wyton R.A.F. Station, Huntingdon.

Royal Naval Air Station post offices are established at Culdrose, Helston, Cornwall, and at Ford, Arundel, Sussex.

Royal Automobile Club
The name of a sub-post office in the South Western Head postal district of London, England.

Royal Courts of Justice
A branch post office in the Western Central Head postal district of London, England.

Royal Postmarks
Date-stamps connected with royalty form an interesting sideline of the postmark hobby. Within this group come such prized possessions as the date-stamps of Buckingham Palace, Balmoral Castle, Holyrood Palace, the Royal Yacht, Sandringham, Windsor Castle and the Royal Pavilion at Aldershot.

Not everyone is aware that such interesting imprints exist. They do, of course, and since Royal correspondence is considerable it follows that the number of Royal postmarks in circulation is relatively higher than might be imagined.

Special postal markings have been used on many occasions in connection with overseas visits made by various members of the British Royal Family. A special postmark, now rare, was used at the Coronation Durbar in Delhi in 1911, another, with the Royal Arms incorporated, commemorated the then Prince of Wales' tour of South Africa in 1925 and, in 1934, the visit of Prince George to South and Central

Africa. A special commemorative postmark was used for the Royal visit to Canada in 1939, the words 'Royal Train, Canada' and the Royal Standard being incorporated in the design.

See: 'Balmoral Castle', 'Royal Visit, Basutoland', etc.

Royal visit – Basutoland

Basutoland – sometimes called 'The Switzerland of South Africa' – was one of the territories honoured, in 1947, by a visit of Their Majesties King George VI and Queen Elizabeth, with the two Princesses during their South African tour.

The Royal party left Portsmouth on 1 February 1947 in H.M.S. *Vanguard*, arriving in Cape Town on 17 February. For two months the Royal Family travelled by special train and at Maseru (Basutoland) an elaborate and colourful parade, attended by 100,000 natives, was held in their honour.

The postmark commemorating this part of the Royal tour is one of several connected with British Royalty.

'Rugby Shoe'

A scarce and unusual type of postmark in use at Rugby (Warwickshire, England) about 1857.

'Running Chicken' cancellation

A curious pictorial cancellation, now rare, in use at Waterbury, Connecticut, U.S.A., about 1869. It depicted a chicken running with wings outspread.

S

Saar Territory (Number of Post Offices)

On 11 October 1947 the people of the Saar territory, French Zone of Germany, voted for economic union with France.

In 1952 post offices in the area under French jurisdiction numbered 396.

St. Andrew's Cross postmark
A rare Scottish cancellation in use in Edinburgh in the 1880s. It consisted of a circular date-stamp combined with an obliterator of four heavy bars intersected with diagonal cuts and containing the numerals '131'.

St. Christopher and Nevis (Number of Post Offices)
With Anguilla, became members of the West Indies Federation, within the British Commonwealth, in 1958.

Post Offices (1952) including dependencies: eight.

St. Helena (Number of Post Offices)
An island colony in the south Atlantic.

There was one post office on the island in 1952.

St. Helena joined the Universal Postal Union in 1896.

St. Kilda
An island of the Outer Hebrides, Scotland, some 60 miles from the larger Island of Harris; its inhabitants were evacuated on 5 September 1930.

Letters were often sent from the tiny island by means of the 'St.Kilda Mailboat' – the 'mailboat ' being a small piece of wood, hollowed out to allow a small bottle, containing the letter, to be placed inside it. A lid was added bearing the words 'St. Kilda Mail: Finder Please Post', the lid then being nailed over the cavity and an inflated sheep's bladder was then attached to aid the 'mailboat's' progress.

Letters so posted were often recovered from the sea off the Norwegian coast after which they were forwarded to London for redirection. Four out of every six letters posted in this way were said to have reached their destination.

The island possessed an official post office and on the day before the island was evacuated, in 1930, the postmaster and his helpers handled the biggest outgoing mail in the island's history to meet hundreds of requests for postmarks.

158

St. Pierre and Miquelon (Number of Post Offices)
French overseas territory comprising eight small islands off the south coast of Newfoundland.

In 1952 there were three post offices in the territory.

St. Vincent (Number of Post Offices)
Became a member of the West Indies Federation within the British Commonwealth in 1958.

Number of post offices in the group (including dependencies) in 1952: twenty-seven.

In 1852 the General Post Office (U.K.) opened a branch office in St. Vincent. The island joined the Universal Postal Union in 1881.

Sandflats
In 1956 a Port Elizabeth city councillor, Mr. A. Barris, became the sole owner of Sandflats, a village in Cape Province, South Africa, about fifty miles from Port Elizabeth. He bought it for £20,500.

The village includes a licensed hotel, a general dealer's business, garage premises, several houses, a bank and a post office.

Santa Claus
Scattered here and there about the world are numerous towns and cities whose names reflect the spirit of Christmas in one form or another.

Santa Claus, Spencer county, Indiana, U.S.A., is one such place. It is the only town in the United States so named and the privilege of using the exclusive Santa Claus postmark is reserved to the Indiana post office by Congressional Act.

São Thome and Principe Islands (Number of Post Offices)
Portuguese colony in the Gulf of Guinea.

Number of post offices (1952): eleven.

School and university postmarks
It is surprising how many schools and universities appear in postmark form from sources in various parts of the world.

Representing Great Britain are the date-stamps of Ampleforth College (York), Duke of York's School (Dover, Kent), Owens College (Manchester), and Ushaw College (Durham). Drake Hall, Stafford, a training college for women, also had its own postal imprint until the Hall closed, on 11 February 1950.

Here is a selection of other school and university postmarks obtainable from widely scattered parts of the world. To this list many others could be added:

> Atlantic Christian College, Wilson, North Carolina, U.S.A.
> Brisbane University, Queensland, Australia.
> Victoria School, Pabna, India.
> Wallup State School, Victoria, Australia.
> Debreczen College (400th Anniversary postmark) Czechoslovakia.
> Antigonish University, Nova Scotia, Canada.
> Gujrat College, Ahmedabad, India.
> Niagara University, New York, U.S.A.
> Tufts University, Boston, Massachusetts, U.S.A.

Sea Floor Post Office

Behind the postal imprint 'Sea Floor, Bahamas', lies the story of one of the world's most unusual post offices.

The Sea Floor Post Office was, in fact, a globular, glass-walled chamber built and equipped by Captain John Ernest Williamson of the American Field Museum, for the observation of marine phenomena. Captain Williamson, formerly a cartoonist on the staff of the *Virginia Pilot*, of Norfolk, Virginia, U.S.A., conceived the idea of utilizing, for marine photographic purposes, the flexible metallic tube devised by his father, Charles Williamson, for deep sea salvage and submarine engineering. This tube, which formed an open pathway to the floor of the sea, where it terminated in a steel chamber, was operated through a surface vessel above.

Known as the Williamson Photosphere this remarkable contrivance comprised a well-ventilated undersea studio with an observatory window, the chamber itself being connected by the flexible tube to the pilot craft, *Jules Verne III*, on the ocean surface.

Here, on Wednesday, 16 August 1939, on the sea floor off the Bahamas, in a chamber 6 ft. by 10 ft. at rest in the heart of a marine fairyland, a small company of officials and privileged guests witnessed an event unparalleled in postal history. The Bahamas Sea Floor Post Office – the world's first undersea postal depot – was formally opened.

160

To commemorate this unique event First Day covers were despatched bearing Bahama postage stamps on envelopes autographed by Captain Williamson. The first letters to be posted were addressed to King George VI and President Roosevelt. The envelopes bore an illustration showing the interior of the Photosphere and a photographic view, taken from the interior, showing fearsome marine monsters nosing curiously against the thick plate glass of the observatory window.

Inscribed at the foot of the envelopes were the words 'Posted in Williamson Photosphere at Bottom of Sea' and the oval-shaped postmark carried the words 'Sea Floor, Bahamas'.

Secretary

Secretary, in Dorchester county, Maryland, U.S.A., derives its name from George Calvert, first Lord Baltimore, who entered the British Parliament in 1609 and was appointed Secretary of State in 1619.

Lord Baltimore was strongly concerned with colonization and himself visited Newfoundland in 1627 and later sailed southwards in attempts to settle Virginia.

The house in which Lord Baltimore lived at Secretary, Maryland, is still in existence and is owned by the Catholic Church. The inside furnishings and staircase of the original building are now in New York Museum.

Seldom Come By

A community in St. John's postal district, Newfoundland.

Seychelles Islands (Number of Post Offices)

A British colony comprising a group of ninety-two islands in the Indian Ocean.

In 1952 there were five post offices in the colony.

Shellal-Halfa T.P.O.
A travelling post office mail service operated in Egypt.

Short place-names

There are quite a number of two-letter place-names in the world at some of which post offices are established. It follows that an entertaining collection of two-letter place-names can be developed by the enterprising specialist collector.

Ae (Dumfries-shire, Scotland) is one example of a short place-name; Ka (Virginia, U.S.A.), abbreviated in postmark form to Ka, Va., is another. Ti, a two-letter place-name in Oklahoma, U.S.A., derives its brief name from the reversed initial letters of Indian Territory, the former name of the state of Oklahoma.

Other postal place-names noted for their brevity are:

> Au (the name of several small communities in Austria, Germany and Switzerland).
> Ba (Fiji and Ghana).
> Go (Japan).
> Ii (Finland).
> Is (Sverdlovsk, U.S.S.R.).
> Ko (Japan).
> Li (Norway and Thailand).
> Lo (West Flanders, Belgium).
> Lu (Graubunden, Switzerland).
> Mo (Norway).
> Na (Bergen, Norway).
> Oi (there are eight post offices bearing this name in Japan).
> Ro (Denmark, Italy and Sweden).
> Sa (Portugal and Thailand).
> Ut (Kirov, U.S.S.R.).
> Va (Norway and Sweden).

Ye (Amherst, Burma).
Yi (Uruguay).

At one time four American towns bore names which consisted only of two initial letters. They were A.I. (Ohio), O.K. (Kentucky), T.B. (Maryland), and U.Z. (Kentucky). The post offices at these four towns are no longer in existence.

Sierra Leone (Number of Post Offices)
A British colony and protectorate of West Africa.

The first post office was established at Freetown in 1853. About 1937 there were approximately seventy post offices or agencies established and in 1952 there were ninety-six post offices.

Silver Bell
A desert town of 300 families in Pima county, Arizona, U.S.A. There are various stories about the origin of the town's name. The most likely one is that Silver Bell was the name of a near-by silver mine, now disused.

Six
The township of Six, McDowell county, West Virginia, U.S.A., derives its name from the near-by No. 6 Mine operated by a coal company.

Sleepy Eye
A town in Brown county, Minnesota, U.S.A.

Smallest Post Office

From time to time reports appear in the world's newspapers about the claims of this or that post office to being 'the smallest post office in the world' or, alternatively, to being the smallest post office in some particular region.

Such claims are difficult to investigate. They are even more difficult to authenticate. When supported by details they tend, however, to add considerable interest to the possession of postmarks from the lilliputian offices on whose behalf the claims are made.

Here are some details of small post office claimants, based on Press reports from various sources throughout the world:

Great Britain

In 1934 a Sunday newspaper claimed that the post office at Garsdale Head, Sedbergh, Yorkshire, was the smallest in Britain. The office lay in a dip of the remote Yorkshire fells, 11½ miles from the nearest large centre of population. It measured 9 ft. by 6 ft.

Great Oak, Raglan, Monmouthshire, and Rose Ash, South Molton, Devon, were named, in 1947, as claimants to the title of 'Britain's smallest post office', but no details of dimensions were given.

In September 1952 a London evening newspaper reported: 'The G.P.O. have built their smallest post office in the little village of Twin-stead, near Sudbury, Suffolk. Built of wood it can only hold two people at a time. The average number of customers in a day is twelve.'

Australia

In Australia the 'smallest post office' claim begins with the office at Locksley, New South Wales, which lies 16 miles south-east of Bathurst and serves a population of about fifty people. The dimensions of Locksley's post office, quoted by an Australian magazine in 1958, are 8 ft. 6 ins. by 7 ft. 6 ins.; height 8 ft. 6 ins.

Locksley's claim was challenged, in 1959, by the post office at Bigg's Flat, near Adelaide, South Australia, an office open for short periods only, whose dimensions were quoted as 7 ft. by 5 ft.; height 6 ft. 6 ins.

Probably, however, Australia's 'smallest ever' post office was one formerly established at Lower Cape Bridgewater, Victoria. It was 6 ft. by 4 ft. and had been run for four generations by the Hedditch family. This post office – 12 miles west of Portland – was opened in 1863 and closed in 1953.

U.S.A.

The post office at Bill's Place, Pennsylvania, measured 7 ft. 2 ins. by 4 ft. 11 ins. and was probably at one time the smallest in the U.S.A. It was discontinued in the 1950's.

In 1957 an office measuring 14 ft. by 8 ft. was opened at Cypress Gardens, Florida. Another post office of bandbox dimensions is the wooden structure at Little Orleans, Maryland, which serves a rural community of 600 people.

'Smokey' postmarks
A cartoon character, 'Smokey Bear', who appears on American postmarks and posters exhorting the public to preserve the countryside.

Snaefell summit
A triangular impression sometimes found on letters and postcards posted on the summit of Snaefell Mountain (2,034 ft.), Isle of Man, Great Britain, in use from 1906 or earlier.

A similar imprint is used on letters posted on Snowden summit, North Wales, but neither of these impressions fall within the category of official postal markings.

Solomon Islands Protectorate (Number of Post Offices)
A British Protectorate of the Western Pacific.

Number of post offices in the group (1952): five.

Somaliland (Number of Post Offices)
A British Protectorate of East Africa.

The Somaliland post office was established in 1903. In 1952 there were nine post offices in the territory.

Southern Rhodesia (Number of Post Offices)
A region lying south of the Zambesi River, South Africa. From 1953 became a unit of the Federation of Rhodesia and Nyasaland.
Number of post offices (1952): 161.

Spain (Number of Post Offices)
According to figures issued by the Universal Postal Union the number of post offices in Spain in 1952 was 9,428.

Stamps
Stamps, Lafayette county, Arkansas, U.S.A., was so named in the latter part of 1884 by Mrs. C. T. Crowell, the first postmistress, in honour of her father, James Hardy Stamps, an early settler in the region.

It is now principally a manufacturing town with some farming and considerable oil production. Population: 2,500.

Stepaside
A curious place-name near Narbeth, Pembrokeshire, Wales, where a post office bears this name.

Success
Formerly known as Bridgeford; a small town in Clay county, Arkansas, U.S.A., near the Current River and Missouri stateline.

The story concerning this community's curious name is that at a critical period in the town's history, about the turn of the twentieth century, a crop was sown upon which much depended. Its citizens agreed that if the crop was a success the town should be given this name.

Sudden

A village in south-east Lancashire, England, one mile south-west of Rochdale. The name is probably a corruption of 'South Dene'. Post office established here 1883.

Sweden (Number of Post Offices)

Kingdom of N. Europe.

Number of post offices (1952): 4,734.

Switzerland (Number of Post Offices)

Central European republic comprising a confederation of twenty-two cantons.

Number of post offices (1952): 4,021.

T

Table Mountain

A postmark from an unusual source. Table Mountain (altitude 3,549 ft.) lies in Cape Province, Union of South Africa, just south of Cape Town, overlooking the city and Table Bay. The summit is flat, often shrouded in a white mist called 'the tablecloth'. A cable railway, built in 1929, runs to the summit.

Talking Rock

An interesting tale is told about the origin of the name of this small town, which is situated in Pickens county, Georgia, U.S.A.

According to the legend there was, in the early pioneer days, a large stone beside the trail in this region. On the stone some jokester had written 'Turn me over'.

167

To the accompaniment of a good deal of huffing and blowing and puffing curious folks would turn the stone over, only to discover the words 'Turn me back, that I may fool another' written on the other side.

Later, a town was settled in this region and took its name from 'the talking rock'.

Tanganyika (Number of Post Offices)
Trusteeship territory of East Africa.
Number of post offices (1952): 412.

Tangier
Morocco, North Africa.

The first British post office was established at Tangier, Morocco, in

1857. One hundred years later, on 1 May 1957, 20,000 square feet of British territory in the International Zone of Tangier, on which the post office formerly stood, were handed over to the Sultanate of Morocco.

Until this happened the British Post Office in Tangier was one of the most unusual post offices in the world. Postage stamps could be paid for not only in sterling but in francs, pesetas, roubles, dollars, and even Maria Theresa dollars, for Tangier's status as an international free port allowed the use of any currency. The postmaster was a Scot from Lerwick, in the Shetland Islands, his assistant an Englishman from Bath, Somerset, and the staff consisted of two Moors, two Spaniards, and a Moroccan Jew who spoke English, German, French, Spanish, Arabic, Russian, and Chinese.

Ta-Ta-Creek
A community 10 miles south of the Skookum-chuck ('Good Water') River, British Columbia, Canada.

Said to have derived its name from the derisive farewell of 'Red' McLeod, a badman of the pioneer days, as he escaped from a sheriff's custody.

Ten Sleep
Washakie county, Wyoming, U.S.A.

The isolated town of Ten Sleep lies in north-central Wyoming, near Nowood Creek, in a region of battlegrounds and massacres in the bygone pioneer days. Pop. 289.

Near the town is a large cave which marked the half-way stage between the Indians' summer and winter hunting grounds.

The cave could comfortably sleep ten redskins and from this fact, handed down in legend, Ten Sleep derived its name.

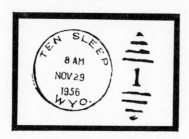

Tenterden
An urban district and market town near Rye, Kent, England. It has a church with a famous steeple. Population: 4,500.

Here, as told by James Lees-Milne, is the outline of a romantic story concerning a postmark of Tenterden, Kent:

Towards the end of the last century, during the most successful stage partnership that this country has ever known, Henry Irving and Ellen Terry were out driving one autumn afternoon. After ambling across the open marshlands between Rye and Tenterden they reached a little bridge that spans a narrow stream. . . .

On their right they saw an old farmhouse of dark, upright timbers, with a sloping red-tiled roof and one large, friendly chimney stack. In her impetuous manner, Ellen Terry called out: 'This is where I should like to live and die.'

'Well, then – buy it!' said Irving.

Inside the house was an old shepherd. Ellen Terry accosted him with: 'Do you live here?'

'No-a.'

'Is this a nice house?'

'No-a.'

'Do you think you will remember me if it ever is for sale?'

'Ye-es.'

Several years later Ellen Terry received a postcard with the words 'House For Sale' and nothing else upon it.

But the postmark was Tenterden.

She took a train at once and hurried there and that is how she bought in 1900, the fifteenth-century house in which she spent so many happy years until her death, at Tenterden, occurred on 21 July 1928.

The

Many postal place-names are prefixed by the 'definite article' – 'The' – and a creditable collection can be made of postmarks from such sources.

Here is a selection of post offices in various parts of the world whose names are prefixed in this way:

The Birches	Portadown, Co. Armagh, Ireland.
The Braes	Portree, Isle of Skye.
The Camp	Stroud, Gloucestershire, England.
The Chart	Oxted, Surrey, England.
The Commons	Thurles, Tipperary, Eire.
The Cross	Lifford, Co. Donegal, Eire.
The Down	Bridgnorth, Shropshire, England.
The Edge	Stroud, Gloucestershire, England.
The Fall	East Ardsley, Wakefield, England.
The Forest	Abergavenny, Monmouthshire.
The Glen	Innerleithen, Peeblesshire, Scotland.
The Green	Millom, Cumberland, England.
The Haven	Billingshurst, Sussex, England.
The Hyde	London, N.W.9, England.
The Lizard	Helston, Cornwall, England.
The Pigeons	Co. Westmeath, Eire.
The Rower	C. Kilkenny, Eire.
The Stone	Southminster, Essex, England.
The Vale	Guernsey, Channel Islands.
The Basin	Victoria, Australia.
The Baths	Cape Province, South Africa.
The Bluff	Harbour Island, Bahamas.
The Bottom	Dutch West Indies.
The Bridge	Queensland, Australia.
The Brothers	Victoria, Australia.
The Caves	Queensland, Australia.
The Chateau	Hamilton, New Zealand.
The Current	Harbour Island, Bahamas.
The Entrance	New South Wales, Australia.
The Forks	Maine, U.S.A.
The Glades	New Brunswick, Canada.

The Gums	Queensland, Australia.
The Head	Queensland, Australia.
The Heart	Victoria, Australia.
The Island	Cape Province, South Africa.
The Lagoon	New South Wales, Australia.
The Maze	Lisburn, Co. Antrim, Ireland.
The Patch	Victoria, Australia.
The Plains	Virginia, U.S.A.
The Point	South Australia.
The Rest	Cape Province, South Africa.
The Ridge	Ontario, Canada.
The Risk	New South Wales, Australia.
The Rock	Georgia, U.S.A.
The Sisters	Victoria, Australia.
The Slash	Ontario, Canada.
The Slopes	New South Wales, Australia.
The Summit	Queensland, Australia.
The Valley	St. Christopher & Nevis, West Indies.
The Willows	New Brunswick, Canada.

Thematic collecting

The harvesting of a thematic group of unusual postmarks can be an amusing and informative pastime. Philatelists frequently collect not only by country but by topic or theme. Doctors, for example, may be attracted to postage stamp scenes depicting medical treatment, hospitals, and healing; connoisseurs of art may be tempted to fill their albums with specimens portraying famous pictures and artists, just as army officers are sometimes drawn to an interest in adhesives dealing with battles and military history.

For the postmark enthusiast opportunities quite as entertaining are offered. As will be seen from sections of this book, groups of postmarks on almost every theme from animals and birds to beverages and bridges can be gathered with the exercise of a little patience and ingenuity and the co-operation of friends and fellow-collectors.

It remains merely for the collector to select a group upon which his interests are most naturally centred and thereafter to begin the absorbingly pleasant recreation of building a worthy collection upon this theme.

Tin Can Canoe Mail

Four hundred miles south-east of Fiji, in the Southern Pacific, is a cluster of islands known as the Friendly, or Tongan, Group.

From Niuafoou, or Tin Can Island, one of the units in this group, in latitude 15° 33′ S. and longitude 175° 39′ W., comes a postmark calculated to echo the words set by Shakespeare upon the lips of Hamlet: *'There are more things in heaven and earth, Horatio, than are dreamt of in your philosophy . . .'*

For at Niuafoou the transport of letters in a metal container from the island to mail steamers (which could not approach the shore owing to the heavy surf) was at one time one of the Seven Wonders of the philatelic world.

In 1939, after eleven years' service as the island postman, Mr. Stuart Ramsey retired. Mr. Ramsey's job consisted of swimming out to steamers through treacherous waters towing behind him a 40-lb. biscuit tin containing the islanders' mail. Later other versions of this service were carried out and the letters thus handled for transmission to the world's far corners were decorated with a truly amazing variety of postal markings.

Today the Niuafoou phenomena is no longer in existence, and one of the problems reported in a Government publication as facing the Tongan authorities was that of the resettlement of the island's 1,300 inhabitants following a disastrous volcanic eruption in September 1945. This catastrophe completely destroyed the Government station, damaged property and food crops, and eventually necessitated evacuation of the population to the neighbouring island of Eua.

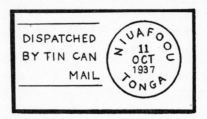

Todmorden

A municipal borough, market, and manufacturing town on the River Calder, and Rochdale Canal, 8¾ miles south-east of Burnley, Yorkshire, England. Population: 21,400.

There are two interesting background facts about the postmark of Todmorden.

One is that business in the town's head post office is conducted in Todmorden Hall, an ancient, gabled building, with mullioned windows, 300-year-old panelling and a chimneypiece dated 1603. The building was formerly the home of the prosperous Radcliffe family whose coat-of-arms is featured on the carved chimneypiece.

The second curious fact is that although works of reference invariably quote Todmorden as being in Yorkshire, the town appears in postmark form as 'Todmorden, Lancs.'.

Togoland (Number of Post Offices)
A self-governing republic within the French Union of West Africa. Post offices (1952): eighteen.

Tombstone
A town in Cochise county, Arizona, U.S.A., near the Mexican border, formerly notorious as a mining camp and the scene of many gun-fights, and now a resort catering for people suffering from rheumatism.

The names of Wyatt Earp, Doc Halliday, and many other well-known characters are associated with Tombstone which is said to have been given its name by a prospector named Schieffelin. Schieffelin was prospecting in the area at a time when the region was infested with Apache Indians. He was warned that all he would find would be his tombstone. Later Schieffelin located one of the richest strikes in the West and when he did so he is credited with the remark: 'Here is my tombstone.'

Adjacent to Tombstone is the famous Boothill cemetery with its stock of curious inscriptions. One reads, laconically, 'Hanged By Mistake'; another carries the inscription 'Died a Natural Death'. A third Tombstone legend, in verse, reads:

> Here lies Les Moore
> Four slugs from a .44
> No Les
> No Moore.

Tombstone's daily newspaper is fittingly named *The Epitaph*.

Tonga (Number of Post Offices)
Also known as the Friendly Islands.
A Protected State of the south Pacific since 1900. A postal system has operated here since 1886. In 1952 there were six post offices.

T.P.O. and Seapost Society
Founded by Mr. J. H. Tierney, of Glasgow, this society caters for collectors interested in postmarks connected with travelling post offices and maritime postmarks.
A bulletin is issued.
Hon. secretary: N. Hill, 34 Old Wortley Road, Rotherham, Yorkshire.

Trans-Atlantic Post Office
Wording formerly used on correspondence posted on board British vessels on Atlantic routes.

Travelling Post Offices
On 6 January 1838, Britain's first travelling post office was established

when a converted horse-box, known as 'the post office van', was attached to a train on the Grand Junction (later the L.M.S.) line.
This enterprise proved to be so successful that in June 1838 a travelling post office was ordered to be specially built.
Today travelling post offices of various kinds are in operation in many parts of the world and are a source of interesting postal markings of varied types.

Trinidad and Tobago (Number of Post Offices)
Part of the West Indies Federation within the British Commonwealth.
The first post office was established in Trinidad in 1801 and a branch of the G.P.O. (U.K.) was installed at Tobago in 1841.
There were 163 post offices functioning in the colony in 1952.

Tristan da Cunha
Discovered by a Portuguese, from whom it took its name, this lonely

South Atlantic island which lies mid-way between Cape Town and South America, has been a British possession since 1816.

For 300 days of the year storms whistle across this tiny piece of land and make crop-growing difficult for the island's 250 hardy inhabitants. Their diet consists largely of potatoes and fish, for visits from passing ships are rare.

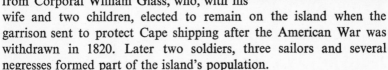

The island's inhabitants are descended from Corporal William Glass, who, with his wife and two children, elected to remain on the island when the garrison sent to protect Cape shipping after the American War was withdrawn in 1820. Later two soldiers, three sailors and several negresses formed part of the island's population.

Today there is a church, a small school, and a hospital on the island whose inhabitants speak English with a quaint, long-forgotten eighteenth-century accent.

Truth Or Consequences

One of the world's most strangely-named places is surely the town of Truth Or Consequences, Sierra county, New Mexico, U.S.A.

Truth Or Consequences (population 4,500) is a health resort in a livestock-rearing and agricultural area of the Rio Grande. Situated at an altitude of 4,200 feet, Its amenities include hot mineral springs and a hospital for the treatment of poliomyelitis.

Formerly known as Hot Springs, its name was changed in 1950 when Ralph Edwards, an American television and radio producer, was planning the tenth anniversary of his successful 'Truth Or Consequences' programme. Edwards suggested that some town might like to adopt the name of his show. The residents of Hot Springs liked the idea: their town was often confused with Hot Springs, Arkansas.

An election was held – and the townsfolk of Hot Springs voted in favour of the new name by 1,294 votes to 295.

Turks and Caicos Islands (Number of Post Offices)
Part of the West Indies Federation, established in 1958.
The first post office was established in the Turks Islands in 1854. In 1952 there were three post offices functioning.

Twelve Mile
The town of Twelve Mile (population 225) lies in farming country on the Chesapeake and Ohio railroad, Cass county, Indiana, U.S.A.
Replying to a correspondent in March 1957, Postmistress Sylvia Swanson wrote:

'I do not know how the town received its name. Some say it was from the little creek near here which is 12 miles long. . . .'

Tynlon
Anglesey, Wales.
Like Brynteg, Anglesey (q.v.), the post office at Tynlon takes its name from the house in which the office is situated. The name of the village in which Tynlon is located is Llynfaes.

Tynygongl
Anglesey, Wales.
Tynygongl is another example of a post office deriving its name from that of a private house. In this case the name of the village is Benllech but for many years the post office has gone by the name of Tynygongl.
See also Brynteg, Anglesey, Wales, and Tynlon, Anglesey, Wales.

176

U

Ugley
A Hertfordshire (England) village whose
inhabitants claim that it is far from ugly!

Union of South Africa (Number of Post Offices)
Number of post offices (1952): 3,497.

United Kingdom (Number of Post Offices)
There are approximately (1959) 24,000 post offices in the United
Kingdom and Northern Ireland.

This figure has remained comparatively static since 1910 when the
number of post offices in the United Kingdom was quoted as 23,775.

Previous figures were:

1860	—	11,412
1888	—	17,587
1899	—	21,940
1952	—	24,510

United States Army Air Force Post Offices
It is possible to build a large collection of postmarks from American
Air Force post offices established in the U.S.A. and overseas stations.

Here is a brief list of some of these postal stations, to which many
others could be added:

Brookley Air Force Base, Alabama.
Brooks Air Force Base, Texas.
Bryan Air Force Base, Texas.
Cannon Air Force Base, New Mexico.
Carswell Air Force Base, Texas.
Chanute Air Force Base, Illinois.

Columbus Air Force Base, Mississippi.
Davis-Monthan Air Force Base, Arizona.
Donaldson Air Force Base, South Carolina.
Dover Air Force Base, Delaware.
Eglin Air Force Base, Florida.
England Air Force Base, Louisiana.
Fairchild Air Force Base, Washington.
Goodfellow Air Force Base, Texas.
Hamilton Air Force Base, California.
James Connally Air Force Base, Texas.
Keesler Air Force Base, Mississippi.
Langley Air Force Base, Virginia.
Mountain Home Air Force Base, Idaho.
Offutt Air Force Base, Nebraska.
Paine Air Force Base, Washington.
Pinecastle Air Force Base, Florida.
Robins Air Force Base, Georgia.
Stead Air Force Base, Nevada.
Tinker Air Force Base, Oklahoma.
Vance Air Force Base, Oklahoma.
Webb Air Force Base, Texas.
Wright-Patterson Air Force Base, Ohio.

United States of America (First Post Office)
The first Federal post office was established in 1776 at 44 Corn Hill, Boston, Massachusetts.

In the same year a post office was established at Ralston, New Jersey.

United States of America (Number of Post Offices)
The total number of post offices in the U.S.A. and associated territories on 1 July 1957 was 37,012.

The breakdown of these figures into states and other regions was as follows:

Alabama	..	..	.. 793	Florida	.. ..	.. 547
Alaska	..	..	.. 227	Georgia	.. ..	.. 768
Arizona	..	..	.. 247	Guam	.. ..	.. 1
Arkansas	..	..	.. 842	Hawaii	.. ..	.. 99
California	..	..	.. 1,357	Idaho	.. ..	.. 348
Canton Island	..	..	1	Illinois	.. ..	.. 1,385
Caroline Islands	..	..	4	Indiana	.. ..	.. 844
Colorado	..	..	.. 489	Iowa	.. ..	.. 1,050
Connecticut	..	..	.. 274	Kansas	.. ..	.. 814
Delaware	..	..	.. 64	Kentucky	.. ..	.. 1,831
Dist. of Columbia		..	1	Louisiana	.. ..	.. 610

Maine	..	 631	Oregon	.. ..	.. 503
Mariana Islands	..	.. 1	Pennsylvania	.. ..	2,177
Marshall Islands	..	.. 1	Puerto Rico	..	.. 105
Maryland ..	..	.. 509	Rhode Island	..	.. 66
Massachusetts	..	.. 543	Samoa ..	.. ..	1
Michigan ..	..	.. 949	South Carolina	..	.. 441
Minnesota ..	..	.. 959	South Dakota	..	.. 497
Mississippi ..	..	.. 578	Tennessee ..	..	.. 676
Missouri ..	..	.. 1,224	Texas	.. ..	1,767
Montana ..	..	.. 471	Utah	.. ..	.. 274
Nebraska ..	..	.. 623	Vermont ..	..	.. 328
Nevada ..	..	.. 117	Virginia ..	..	1,399
New Hampshire	..	.. 313	Virgin Islands	..	.. 5
New Jersey	..	.. 584	Wake Island	..	.. 1
New Mexico	..	.. 418	Washington	..	.. 608
New York	..	.. 1,803	West Virginia	..	1,333
North Carolina	..	.. 882	Wisconsin ..	..	.. 854
North Dakota	..	.. 554	Wyoming ..	..	.. 234
Ohio	..	.. 1,242			
Oklahoma ..	..	.. 745		Total	.. 37,012

In 1901 there were 76,945 post offices in the United States. The total on 1 July 1959 was 35,750.

Universal Postal Union

(Le Bureau International de l'Union Postale Universelle.)

Headquarters: Schosshaldenstrasse 46, Berne, Switzerland.

Established on 9 October 1874 by the Postal Convention of Berne, coming into effect on 1 July 1875, and extended and improved by subsequent Postal Congresses.

The Union was established to alleviate the uncertainty, confusion, and excessive cost of international postal communications by uniting its member countries in a single postal territory for the reciprocal exchange of mail. The Bureau acts as a liaison organ and furnishes information and advice to the countries belonging to the Union. Originally called the General Postal Union, it was renamed the Union Postale Universelle in 1878.

Number of member-countries (1958): ninety-eight.

Unusual place-names

Many of the world's most unusual postal place-names have already been mentioned in these pages but in a work limited by space it is inevitable that thousands of places with equally curious names have been omitted.

To the postmark collector the qualifying question regarding any unusual place-name must be: Has it got a post office? Pity Me, Co. Durham, England, is a fascinating place-name but to the postmark collector it suffers from a drastic deficiency. There is no post office at Pity Me.

This is true, also, of so many of the world's store of incredibly fascinating place-names. Hot Coffee (Mississippi, U.S.A.), Cocked Hat (Yorkshire, England), and Come to Good (Cornwall) are all worthy of inclusion in the collector's files but until post offices are established at these places they must remain, regrettably, unrepresented.

This does not imply that there is any serious deficiency in the number of peculiar postal place-names already available to the enterprising collector. On the contrary there are, throughout the world, far more oddly-named post offices than the individual collector could hope to gather in an average lifetime.

A list of some of these quaintly-named post offices, to which reference has not been made elsewhere in this book, may serve as a guide to the seeker after stimulating place-names whose oddity deserves mention:

Blue Sky	Alberta	Canada
Home Rule	N.S.W.	Australia
Silly	Hainaut	Belgium
Dafter	Michigan	U.S.A.
Pure Gold	Andros	Bahamas
Lazy	Silesia	Poland
Wagga Wagga	N.S.W.	Australia
Badlot	Punjab	Pakistan
Tin-Tin	Coochabamba	Bolivia
Tiny	Krasnoiarsk	U.S.S.R.
Pincushion	Boston, Lincs.	England
Bunny	Nottingham	England
Eyebrow	Saskatchewan	Canada
Whiteness	Lerwick	Scotland
Smiths Turn Out	S. Carolina	U.S.A.
Snook's Arm	Newfoundland	Canada
Baby	Lodz	Poland
Mummie	Kentucky	U.S.A.
Papa	Veszprem	Hungary
Paint Lick	Kentucky	U.S.A.
Dog Pound	Alberta	Canada
Old Joe	Arkansas	U.S.A.
Lucky Strike	Alberta	Canada
Bowlegs	Oklahoma	U.S.A.

Stormy Corner	Lancashire	England
Lion's Head	Ontario	Canada
Playing Place	Cornwall	England
Rumbling Bridge	Kinross-shire	Scotland

Up Down Hill
Up Down Hill is the name of a sub-post office at Windlesham, Surrey, England.

U.S. Cancellation Club, The
The U.S. Cancellation Club is a non-profit-making organization for those interested (beginners or advanced specialists) in the postal markings and cancellations of the United States of America.

Departments of the club include those of exchange, research, and valuation and a bi-monthly magazine is issued to members.

Secretary: C. D. Root, 855 Cove Way, Denver 9, Colorado, U.S.A.

V

Vatican City (Citta del Vaticano)
Here is a postmark of the smallest state in the world: area 108.7 acres. In it is situated the beautiful palace of His Holiness the Pope.

There are six letter boxes in the Vatican State – one of them in the dome of St. Peter's, 160 feet above the famous square – and there are four postmen, two for service within the Vatican City and two who carry out delivery services in the State's extra-territorial property in Rome.

The public post office, where two million lire worth of stamps are sold monthly, serves a population of about 1,000. It has a neat and spotless interior and among its distinguished customers are dignitaries of Church and State, government officials, gendarmes and wealthy foreign visitors.

In spite of its diminutive size nearly a ton of mail leaves this pocket State every day.

Vaudins
The name first given to pillar boxes, after the foundryman who made them.
 The earliest British pillar boxes were hexagonal in shape.
 See: Pillar Box.

Victoria Falls
A post office in Southern Rhodesia bears the name of these famous falls, which were discovered by Dr. Livingstone in 1855.

Viet-Nam (Number of Post Offices)
A state in south-east Asia, formerly within the French Union.
 Number of post offices (1952): ninety-seven.

Voortrekker Monument
A South African commemorative postmark representing the Voortrekker Monument at Pretoria was issued in 1949.

W

Waghorn, Lieut. Thomas
Postal pioneer (1800–1850) born in Rochester, Kent.
 After trials commencing in 1829–30 Waghorn, a former officer with the East India Company, put forward a scheme for improving the mail service to India by means of an overland route across Egypt, between Suez and Alexandria.
 Old covers marked 'Care of Mr. Waghorn' are greatly prized by students of Postal History and are of considerable value.

Wait-a-Bit
A postal place-name in Jamaica, British West Indies.

War and Victory
Some time during the morning or early afternoon of Sunday, 3 September

1939, someone popped a letter into the mailbox of a small West Virginian township.

The name of the township was War.

On that same day, several thousand miles away, the people of Britain heard on their radio sets the measured tones of their Prime Minister, Mr. Neville Chamberlain, telling them that they were at war with Nazi Germany.

About five-and-a-half years later, in the state of Vermont, U.S.A., another letter started on its journey. The date was 8 May 1945, on which day, at one minute past midnight, the war in Europe had ended. The place at which this letter was posted also had a curious name.

It was called Victory.

The postal markings borne by these two letters are reproduced below. They are probably – almost certainly – unique.

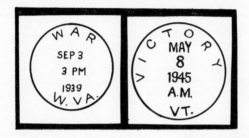

Washington's Birthplace

Washington's Birthplace is the name of a permanent post office in Westmorland county, Virginia, U.S.A.

The name commemorates the fact that George Washington, first President of the United States of America, was born here on 22 February 1732.

Waterbury cancellations

Several different types of unusual hand-cancellers were in use at Waterbury, Connecticut, U.S.A., from about 1865 to 1869, with occasional instances of later use.

The cancellers were cut by John William Hill (1836–1921), a clerk at Waterbury post office, and became philatelically famous on account of their unusual subjects and unorthodox design.

183

They were cut from cork and featured such subjects as a running chicken, an eagle, an elephant, a heart (for St. Valentine's Day cancellations), and a clown's head (for use on 1 April).

The United States postal authorities expressed disapproval of Hill's cancellers on the grounds that they were not dignified enough for official use. Examples of Hill's Waterbury cancellations are now highly prized by collectors.

Welsh place-names

In spite of their formidable appearance to a person unfamiliar with the language, Welsh postal place-names are full of interest and well worth patient study and the effort necessary to translate them.

The name Bettws-y-Coed (North Wales), for example, represents 'house in the wood' and Pontypridd (Glamorgan) = 'bridge of clay'.

What Cheer

What Cheer (originally called Petersburg) in Keokuk county, Iowa, U.S.A., owes its unusual name to the phrase used by early English settlers in the 1870s.

The community was founded in 1865. Immigrants from the north-east regions of England greeted one another on the streets of Petersburg with the words 'What cheer!' meaning 'How are you?' or 'How do you do?'

The greeting captured the imagination of those who sought for the new township a name which was unlikely to be duplicated, so Petersburg became What Cheer.

World's End

A hamlet 6 miles north of Newbury, Berkshire, England, and, postally, a sub-post office of Reading, Berkshire.

There is also a post office named World's End Creek, in South Australia.

184

Worry

The name of a post office established in North Carolina, U.S.A., in the 1930s.

No longer in existence.

Wotton-under-Edge

A market town (population 3,500) near Stroud, Gloucestershire, England.

The Maltese Cross obliteration in use at Wotton-under-Edge in the 1840s has become a star among philately's classics. Its originality lies in the fact that some long-forgotten postmaster heavily scored his stamp obliterator with a series of cross-cuts, presumably with a file or similar tool.

Wreck covers

A philatelic term used to indicate postal material salvaged from mail-carrying vessels involved in accidents and shipwreck.

Such material often carries special postal markings in the form of handstamped or manuscript lettering bearing such inscriptions as 'Saved from the wreck of the *Schiller*', 'Damaged through immersion in sea water', 'Wet through collision on the Nile', etc.

Items of this type often have considerable rarity value and should invariably be retained 'entire'.

X

Postmarks from places whose names begin with 'X' are among the most difficult to find. In 1951 there were only 70 post offices throughout the world classified under this letter. Of these, 26 were in Mexico, 10 in Brazil, and 7 in France. Cyprus and Greece came next: they both had 6 post offices whose names began with 'X', and there were 3 in the U.S.A.

The remaining 12 'X' post offices were in Belgium, Indo-China, and the Union of South Africa (2 each), and Germany, Portuguese West Africa, Spanish Morocco, Mozambique, Italy and Portuguese Guinea (1 each).

Y

Yellowstone National Park
Wyoming, U.S.A.

Largest and most celebrated national park in the U.S.A. It is a government reservation and has an area of 3,350 square miles. Famous for its wild scenery and geysers.

Yosemite National Park
California, U.S.A. Contains magnificently wild scenery; occupies some 1,500 sq. miles.

Z

Zagazig
An important cotton centre and town of about 40,000 inhabitants, with a post office, north of Cairo, Egypt.

Zanzibar (Number of Post Offices)
A Protectorate of East Africa, including the island of Pemba.

A post office was first established here in 1875. In 1952 there were ten post offices operating in the Protectorate.

Zebra
A post office in Cape Province, Union of South Africa.

Zennor
Near St. Ives, Cornwall. Alphabetically speaking, the last postal place-name in the British Isles.

Zero
A township in eastern Montana, U.S.A.

Zigzag
A small town in Clackamas county, Oregon, U.S.A., which received its name from the zigzag formation of a nearby mountain range.

Zyznow
In alphabetical sequence Zyznow, in Poland, is the last postal place-name in the world.

Bibliography

BIBLIOGRAPHY

HERE is a list of some books and official publications which either deal with the postmark collecting hobby or are of use as part of the equipment of the collector. Some of the books listed are out of print but most of them can be obtained from libraries or second-hand bookshops.

History of British Postmarks by J. H. Daniels. (L. Upcott Gill, London, 1898.)

History of the Early Postmarks of the British Isles (to 1840) by J. C. Hendy. (L. Upcott Gill, London, 1905.)

History of the Postmarks of The British Isles from 1840 to 1876 by J. C. Hendy. (Stanley Gibbons Ltd., 1909.)

The Postmarks of Great Britain and Ireland by R. C. Alcock and F. C. Holland. (R. C. Alcock Ltd., Cheltenham.)

British Post Office Numbers (*1844–1906*) by George Brumell. (R. C. Alcock Ltd.)

Local Posts of London (*1680–1840*) by George Brumell. (R. C. Alcock Ltd., 1939.)

The Postmark Slogans of Great Britain by George Brumell. (R. C. Alcock Ltd.)

Postmarks of the British Isles by George Brumell. (Published 1930.)

Irish T.P.O.'s (*Travelling Post Offices*) by C. W. Ward. (Published 1938 from Keston Lodge, Tavistock Road, Croydon.)

Scottish T.P.O.'s by C. W. Ward.

Post Offices in the United Kingdom. (H.M. Stationery Office, York House, Kingsway, London, W.C.2.)

London Post Offices and Streets. (H.M. Stationery Office.)

G.P.O. by E. T. Crutchley. (Cambridge University Press, 1938.)

The Postmark On A Letter by R. K. Forster. (W. & R. Chambers Ltd., 1952.)

The British Post Office by C. F. Dendy Marshall. (Humphrey Milford, Oxford University Press, 1926.)

191

Obliterations and Marques Postale des États-Unis by Michael Zareski. (Published from 45 Boulevard Gouvion-Saint-Cyr, Paris, 17.)

The Tale of the Kicking Mule by Lee H. Cornell. (Published from 1420 Garland Avenue, Wichita, Kansas, U.S.A.)

Britain's Post Office by Howard Robinson. (Oxford University Press, 1953.)

The Stamp Collector's Encyclopaedia by R. J. Sutton. (Hutchinson Scientific & Technical Publications, 1951.)

Haste, Post, Haste! by George Walker. (G. Harrap & Co. Ltd., 1938.)

Handstruck Postage Stamps of the Empire by Robson Lowe. (Herbert Joseph Ltd., 1937.)

The Mails by H. N. Soper. (Universal Postal Frankers Ltd., London.)

Penny Postage Centenary. (Published by the Postal History Society, London, W.1.)

Dictionnaire des Bureau de Poste. In 2 vols. (Universal Postal Union, Berne, Switzerland.)

Stamps of Great Britain (Part I) by J. B. Seymour. (Royal Philatelic Society, London, 1934.)

The Columbia Lippincott Gazetteer of the World. (Columbia University Press, 1952.)

Chambers's World Gazetteer. (W. & R. Chambers Ltd., 1954.)

The Survey Gazetteer of the British Isles. (John Bartholomew & Son Ltd., 1950.)

Census, 1951 (Index of place-names). (H.M. Stationery Office, 1955.)